VITAL PREACHING

The Art of Sharing God's Word

Dr. Justin W. Tull

Copyright 2015

Vital Preaching: The Art of Sharing God's Word
Copyright 2015 © Justin W Tull
All rights Reserved

Requests for permission should be addressed to
justinwtull@yahoo.com

ISBN: 150256016x
ISBN-13: 978-1502560162
Scripture Quotations, unless otherwise indicated, are from New Revised Standard
Version Bible, Copyright 1989
National Council of the Churches of Christ in the United States of America.
Used by permission. All rights reserved.

TABLE OF CONTENTS

INTRODUCTION

ACKNOWLEDGEMENTS

I am deeply indebted to many persons for the production of this book. My first tribute is to Fred Craddock who, more than any other, has shaped both my understanding and practice of preaching by his abundant gifts as scholar, homiletician, and practitioner. Preaching today would be greatly diminished without his extensive and valuable contributions to the field.

I am also grateful for those who have offered much needed technical assistance. Aaron Stout has been my able guide for layout and design, providing both direct assistance and training. Without his valuable partnership I could not have tackled my last four books in such rapid succession.

The essential proofing function of this book has been shared by Karen Long, Margaret Jarvis, and my wife, Janette. Milton Guttierrez has willingly served as the practitioner entrusted to assess the book's teaching value and to offer suggestions when needed.

Most of all, I am indebted to my wife, Janette, whose encouragement, companionship, and loving support has provided for me a nurturing atmosphere in which to both work and write. She has read every word I have written and offered wise counsel and crucial feedback at every major juncture along the way. I will always be grateful for her immense role in all my writing endeavors.

INTRODUCTION

I am convinced that preaching is vitally important to the life and health of the church and as such should be approached with all the resources, skills, and spiritual fervor the preacher can employ. Preaching is not an archaic vehicle for proclamation, as some would suggest, but rather an ongoing practice of some effectiveness, especially if its messenger fulfills such a task with reverence, diligence, and imagination.

Many other professions use peer review as a way to hone their professional skill. Massage therapists regularly exchange massages in order to both give and receive valuable feedback. Voice teachers often invite another musician to listen to their students and give their suggestions concerning vocal technique. Unfortunately, the sermons that most preachers hear are their own. Only on rare occasions are preachers able to experience the gifts and graces of other clergy. Equally limiting is the fact that preachers receive very few candid comments concerning their preaching except those coaxed from a reluctant family member. Often a preacher's main source of evaluation is relegated to the well-meaning comments of the congregation upon leaving the service. "Good job, preacher!" "That was a great sermon!" "You were really talking directly to me." These are all encouraging words but they often give no clue as to what actually made the sermon "good," if, indeed, the comment was totally honest in the first place.

With such limited assessment, a preacher must become very intentional in order to improve the art of preaching. One has to decide to work on the craft and do so, not as an unaccompanied endeavor, but with the help of scholars, the person in the pew, honest self-assessment, and hopefully some peer feedback whenever possible.

Throughout my ministry I have constantly sought ways to grow as a preacher: attending national and local preaching events, being a part of a preaching academy, getting a Doctor of Ministry degree in preaching, teaching preaching for course of study pastors, and in general trying to hone the preaching craft the best I could. All of these deliberate efforts have been helpful, but some of my breakthroughs have come from persons outside the field or simply from a personal "aha" moment in the midst of pastoral ministry. My conclusion is that improving one's preaching is a life-long journey requiring "all the help we can get" including that graciously bestowed by the Holy Spirit.

This book is an effort to reflect critically on the theology and practice of preaching not so much to improve my own offerings, which have been limited since retirement, but to share my insights and practical strategies with preachers who have many sermons yet ahead of them. My goal is to encourage vital preaching across the church. I am convinced that the act of preaching is worthy of our very best efforts using every gift we have and setting aside adequate time in order to do justice to this high calling. Indeed, preaching can change lives, instill hope, challenge complacency, champion justice, and foster compassion. It can address issues that are threatening to overwhelm our church members, those creating doubt, anxiety or uncertainty. Someone needs to say a word: a comforting word, a prophetic word, a word of clarity amidst confusion. I, for one, nominate the preacher.

I do not offer this book as an academic ttextbook on preaching, though there is significant research within its pages. My goal, rather, is to provide a concise and practical overview of preaching, concentrating on all the essential elements of the craft. This book could well be used to introduce the art of preaching to those just beginning the journey or as a "refresher course" to preaching veterans. My hope is that all who read it will discover new ways to enhance their preaching and renew their commitment to excellence in both preparation and execution. Congregations across our nation anxiously await such a renewal. They long for a word that addresses their deepest needs while inviting them into a realm of greater faith and greater faithfulness.

CHAPTER ONE

RULES OF ENGAGEMENT

THE PREACHER'S JOB DESCRIPTION

I have never heard of a single congregation that did not want, if not expect, a good preacher. Most congregations and most individuals can judge whether or not they have a good preacher, but few, if asked, could provide an adequate job description for the task of preaching. Unless a minister can discover an understanding of the preaching task, he or she is totally dependent on the subjective assessment of individuals within the congregation. What minister wants to ask after each sermon "Well, did I preach, really preach, the Word of God this morning"? To avoid such vulnerable inquiry, I have formulated a job description for preaching. This job description includes both the preacher's "task" and "posture."

THE PREACHER'S TASK

It is not easy to define the task of preaching. At the risk of oversimplification, I will endeavor to capture the essence of preaching under two headings: "Telling the Story" and "Interpreting Scripture and Life."

TELLING THE STORY

The phrase that has been the most helpful to me in describing the preacher's task has been "telling the story." This phrase is not without distinguished company—Steimle, Niedenthal, Taylor, and Rice, to name a few. It was Dr. Zan Holmes, however, who provided for me the most concise definition of preaching. Preaching is to "share God's story, so that it becomes the preacher's story, so that it may become the congregation's story."[1] Barbara Brown Taylor in her book, *The Preacher's Life*, shares her perspective on story:

> The stories I tell from the pulpit are not just "my" stories but "our" stories which are God's stories too. The stool of my sermon rests evenly on these three legs. If any one of them is missing (or too long or too short), the whole thing will wobble and fall.[2]

It is Charles Rice, however, who formulates this trilogy of story in all its complexity. His discussion becomes an insightful commentary and expansion of the two statements made above:

> . . . (1) the biblical story, apart from which there would be no preaching; (2) the preacher's own individual story, through which the biblical story is filtered and which adds the preacher's own individual witness that the biblical story has in fact become the preacher's story; (3) the story of the listeners, the community of believers, who have provided the place and occasion for preaching and who have called the preacher to do on their behalf what the preacher has been trained by them to do—to so interpret the biblical story that light is shed on all three stories.[3]

So it is that the preaching task, far from being a "solo" venture is in fact an act in the midst of a community, one inhabited not only by mere mortals but also graced by the presence of the Creator. To tell the story in such a sacred setting, the preacher should well be humbled. The One for whom the whole story is written and spoken is at hand.

INTERPRETING SCRIPTURE AND LIFE

If "Telling the Story" describes what a preacher does, the next task is to discover the "fields" from which the sermon must be harvested. One of the fields is no surprise: the Scriptures. The second arena is not as obvious: life itself. Clyde Fant underscores the importance of both of these sources: "The preaching of the word of God is the interpretation of an historical event to a contemporary situation by (one) who must be intimately familiar with both."[4]

The preacher must first be an interpreter of Scripture. If there is no effort in this area, if no care is taken to address the Bible and to be addressed by it, then the word shared may indeed be relevant, but it can hardly be called a sermon. A message that has no grounding in the Bible can be *a* word but never *The* Word.

A proper interpretation begins by listening, for how can one interpret what is not heard? The process continues with study and reflection in an effort to understand the word spoken in a different time and place. At some point the preacher must wrestle with how the biblical story intermeshes with his or her story. Interpretation begins as the preacher translates the biblical language into the language of the current culture. In that process the preacher not only interprets; the preacher and the culture may also be radically "interpreted" by the Scripture.

The second level of interpretation comes at the point of "application" or "intersection" between the biblical word and the present situation. Even if the preacher is an excellent exegete, even if he or she has been able to extract the original meaning of the text, the resulting sermon will be of little consequence if the preacher fails to address the present reality along with the hopes, dreams, and anxieties of the congregation. Grady Davis supports this notion: "Thus the preacher is going to be an interpreter of life, as much as is a novelist, playwright, sculptor, painter, columnist or musician, whether he wants to or not, whether he knows it or not."[5]

The preacher therefore is one who tells a story, but only after hearing The Story. That story must then be interpreted and applied to the preacher's own life and to the lives of the congregation. A congregation should well be disappointed if, after hearing the sermon, they have not received God's Story. They will be equally short changed if they have been unable to hear *their* story. A preacher's task is never complete without fulfilling the two-fold task of interpreting the Bible and life itself.

THE PREACHER'S POSTURE

In order for the preacher to be an adequate interpreter of the Bible and life, the proper posture must be used. The body language must be that of "leaning forward" with a hand to the ear. The preacher's spirit must be open to God's presence and willing to engage the emotions. The preacher must be careful not only to tell the story but also to tell it as an *insider*, as one involved. William Willimon suggests that the congregation wants the minister to know their story before telling his or her story. He says, "The congregation believes that ultimately only the one who has faithfully exercised the right to listen has the right to speak."[6] The preacher, therefore, must listen, think, and feel. The preacher's entire experience becomes the raw material from which the sermon is sculpted.

MEDITATION BEFORE PROCLAMATION

Dr. Fred Craddock in *As One without Authority* provides us with an important insight: "The Word of God precedes us; certainly we interpret, but first we listen."[7] Craddock is correct to suggest that the primary task of the preacher is to listen to the text. If one approaches the Bible with conclusions already fixed, then the text will have little to say to the preacher and the preacher, in turn, will have little to say to the congregation.

Most often the sermon process begins with a particular text; in which case the preacher must approach the passage open to new insights. On other occasions the preacher may begin with a human concern or problem and then go in search of a text or texts that address that issue. Extra caution must be taken in these circumstances to insure that the text does not become servant of the issue but rather the issue remains secondary to the text. If the preacher is to be a faithful interpreter, Scripture must always have prominence so that the preacher's words will be more fitting for the pulpit than the inferior platform of the soapbox.

PEW BEFORE PULPIT

The art of listening is not to be reserved exclusively for Scripture. The preacher must be able to perceive the action of God in the midst of daily life. As a preacher learns to "listen" to the congregation, the distance between the pulpit and pew is narrowed and the *preacher's* story is more likely to be *their* story.

Mitchell suggests that the preacher should make every effort to "sit where they sit."[8] Indeed, unless the preacher projects some identification with those in the pew, how can a relevant word be preached, and if preached, how can it be understood? Many experts in the field of preaching suggest that a practical way to include the pew in the pulpit is to imagine the sermon being addressed to individuals within the congregation, people with various theologies, various needs. Frederick Buechner in his book, *Telling the Truth*, describes a slice of humanity gathered before the preacher:

> In the front pews the old ladies turn up their hearing aids, and a young lady slips her six year old a Lifesaver and a

Magic Marker. A college sophomore home for vacation, who is there because he was dragged there, slumps forward with his chin in his hand. The vice-president of a bank who twice that week has seriously contemplated suicide places his hymnal in the rack. A pregnant girl feels the life stir inside her...[9]

As interpreters of life, preachers must never become mere casual observers, taking quick snapshots or selfies to illustrate a thought or idea. Instead, preachers are to be intimately involved in the lives of people. These poignant encounters will serve as ample vignettes to enrich preaching not simply as sermon illustrations but also as insights into the "big picture" of life itself. Many may still expect preachers to be experts in the Bible, but few expect us to be experts of life. Too often we have failed to be honest and accurate interpreters of life and culture. Some have even chosen to see life through "rose-colored" glasses and then try to sell such pretty photoshopped renderings to those in the pew. Only the naïve and wishful parishioner will accept such a portrait of life. The preacher, however, does have a lens that promises to be illuminating. Why not view daily life through the lens of the biblical faith bringing into focus that which has lasting value and relegating to the background the superficial, trite, and mundane? Now that is an interpretation of life worth sharing!

As *insiders* to life experience, preachers understand that they are fellow sojourners in life, not front-and-center deliverers leading people to the secular promise land. Thomas Long shares a similar word with the added touch of convicting humor:

We (preachers) are not visitors from clergy-land, strangers from an unknown land, ambassadors from seminary-land, or even, as much as we may cherish the thought, prophets from wilderness land. We are members of the body of Christ, participants in the worshipping assembly, commissioned to preach by the very people to whom we are about to speak.[10]

As interpreters of life and faith, only one voice will speak, but through that voice, the cries, doubts, hopes and faith of all gathered may well be heard. Preaching, if done correctly, will not be heard as *solo*, but as *symphony*.

A MATTER OF THE HEART

In his book, *The Recovery of Preaching*, Mitchell gives another warning worth heeding: "Preaching needs to be aimed at the whole person and not primarily at the intellect."[11] He insists that one of the elements often missing in white Protestant preaching is emotion. Rational discourse has dominated to the detriment of matters of the heart. To move again into the mainstream of the whole person will not be an easy journey for present-day preaching. Craddock is correct when he says, "The longest trip a person takes is that from head to heart."[12]

But even if preaching needs more emotion, it does not need emotionalism or sentimentality. We do not need more "touching illustrations" but rather sensitivity to the immense richness of life in all its dimensions. Buechner illustrates the difference between *sensitivity* and *sentimentality* as the difference between "savoring" rather than "suffering the sadness of it," or between "sighing over the prettiness of it" rather than "trembling at the beauty of it . . ."[13] Preaching should engage the inner feelings of the listener. If the strings of the heart are not in some way set into motion, it is unlikely that the sermon will produce either music or movement in the hearer.

THE SERMON'S PLACE

In the first section of this chapter, we explored the job description of the preacher, citing both the "task" and the "posture." In this next section, our attention will turn to the sermon itself. We begin with the sermon's formation and then turn to its context and finally assess its authority and purpose.

GIFT OR ART?

It is a difficult task for the preacher to determine how to share credits for the sermon. Is the sermon the pure word of God simply bestowed on one of God's servants? Is the sermon simply the work of a craftsman dependent upon human skills and insights? The truth lies somewhere in between these two questions, for preaching, properly understood, is both gift and art.

AS GIFT GIVEN

The sermon should first be understood as a gift for the sermon begins with the raw material of the gospel itself. Hardin shares a humbling thought for the preacher: "It is essential that we keep in mind the fact that we are preachers to the people not because we have such splendid ideas, but because we have been called by the Church to preach a Word that we didn't have to think up."[14]

The sermon is gift partially because one receives the Scriptures as a gift, but there is more. When the preacher is truly open to that Word, when the preacher is sensitive to the depth of life's experiences, then an idea, a concept, an insight may suddenly come into the preacher's consciousness. Many might call this occurrence just the preacher's own "brilliance." Often it is simply a "gift." I have at times felt uninspired only to suddenly experience the stirring of mind or heart as a fresh idea

12

came to me. Creation is repeated; across the void the Spirit of God moves, and an idea is born.

AS ART CREATED

The gift that comes, however, is never in its final form. Some preachers, I know, claim that their words are simply God's Word. In this way of thinking divine revelation is not only absolute but also instantaneous. The minister need not prepare or wrestle or think, but only open the mouth at the time of proclamation. I reject such "lip-sync" notions of preaching. Instead, I would suggest that a sermon becomes a sermon only when it has the preacher's fingerprints on it. If one looks closely one might also discover, sweat, tearstains, and a smudge of midnight oil.

The sermon is intended to be a joint venture: God providing the raw materials and many of the tools; the preacher providing the talent (a gift itself), energy and a part of his or her being. Thus understood, the sermon is more than a product created by technique. It is a personal offering, one not only acceptable because of the humble spirit with which it is shared but also made more effective by discipline and energy skillfully employed. A great work of art has many of the characteristics of a good sermon. It reflects the uniqueness of the artist. It also speaks deeply to the innermost niches of the human soul.

The call for excellence from the pulpit is a call for the preacher to understand his or her work as that of an artist. It is not a misuse of the office to use poetic finesse, dramatic flair, and imagination to tell *The Story*. Indeed, to neglect any skill or technique in preaching is to shirk not only opportunity but also responsibility. My hunch is that many preachers fail to use an artist's touch more out of ignorance than laziness. Perhaps they do not understand the necessity of crafting the sermon skillfully and lovingly. Perhaps they have foolishly buried their two

13

talents in the ground, thinking them too limited or too secular to be used for the spiritual realm. Craddock has a confronting word for such neglence. He suggests that style and execution are important for every minister because "art is not a gift which few people are given, but rather it is a gift which most people throw away."[15]

THE SERMON'S CONTEXT

Having discussed the sermon as gift and art, we turn to the question of context. Of course, the obvious context of the sermon is biblical tradition. Either the sermon stands inside the biblical context or it fails to qualify as a sermon. Since much time has already been devoted to the biblical grounding of the sermon, other contexts can now be explored that will impact the perspective, if not the content, of the sermon.

IN THE MIDST OF WORSHIP

As a preacher it is difficult to imagine the sermon in any context other than worship. To be sure, I have heard several "sermonic" lectures that had no elements of worship either before or after them. But without elements of worship present, the message is often called a "lecture" rather than a "sermon." To be sure, a message given without other elements of worship is not the same message as when it is shared within a worshipping community.

If one accepts the notion that the sermon is intended to be a part of a worship service, a strong case can be made for the sermon being closely linked to other elements of the worship service. A sermon should acknowledge the spirit or content of that which precedes it and follows it. For example, a sermon preached on communion Sunday might have a different ending than if it were followed by a hymn of praise. I personally strive to coordinate the liturgy, music, and prayers so that they reflect the message or tone of the sermon. Such a method may narrow the scope of the service, but it can well increase its impact. Thus understood, the sermon does not become the only "Word" heard. Rather, the sermon, like the anthem and liturgy, seeks to proclaim God's Word in a way that will address the whole person. It is better that a parishioner says, "That was an excellent service," than "That was an excellent sermon." Even so, as a preacher I must confess I enjoy hearing the latter more!

TO AND FOR THE COMMUNITY OF FAITH

The sermon, if it is to be relevant, must be addressed to all those gathered. Such discourse should not be condescending but rather reflect an understanding of the church member. Thus it is a true compliment when a church member exclaims as she is shaking the minister's hand: "You really were talking to me this morning!"

There is, however, another way the sermon is tied to the listener. The preacher may speak not only "to" the church member but also "for" the church member. When the truth is proclaimed, a truth deeply believed by the member, a sense of identification occurs. The preacher has not simply told *The Story* or *his* or *her* story; but *their* story. Though the preacher seems to be sharing a solo, the congregation is allowed to join in the chorus. It occurs to me that this is precisely the function of the "Amen!" in more expressive congregations. The preacher has spoken a word that they, too, would speak. The preacher has told "their story!" "Amen!"

THE SERMON'S PURPOSE

In his book *The Servant of the Word*, H. H. Farmer asserted that the most distinctive function of a minister is to "produce, preserve, and utilize a sound theology."[16]

RESIDENT THEOLOGIAN

I have long understood one of my primary roles as preacher is to be "resident theologian." Whether I am proclaiming the good news in the message of a memorial service or preaching a sermon following a national tragedy, I will always endeavor to say a biblical word and an existential word that rings true to the Scriptures and the current experiences of life. Being "resident theologian" does not mean I impose my theology on the congregation, but that I oversee the process of inquiry. The sermon is the main place where the congregation can be invited to do theological wrestling. One over-riding purpose or goal of my preaching is that it will be a catalyst for the formation of a mature faith in the listener, one that can sustain itself in the midst of hardship and tragedy. Such a goal is dependent on the biblical faith being shared with theological soundness and at the same time being consistent with the varied experiences of life. The preacher would do well to ask of every text, "What does this passage say about God and our relationship to the Creator? Likewise, as the sermon is being created, the same question needs to be raised as to the sermon's own theology. In addition one might also ask, "What does this sermon suggest about our relationship to our neighbor and to the events of our present-day experience?"

To Increase Faith and Faithfulness

As important as being a catalyst for sound theology is, it does not suffice as my ultimate purpose in preaching. A good theology does not always translate into right living. If forced to give one succinct purpose for my preaching it would be "to increase faith and faithfulness." It has long been my desire to help the listener grow in the faith. The sermon is offered in order to foster a growing relationship with God in Christ and to broaden the listener's understanding of the faith. Even so, the sermon's ultimate purpose is not fully realized until it encourages the person, now growing in understanding and trust, to live out that renewed faith in acts of faithfulness. Thus sermons that never challenge the listener to action have forfeited part of the sermon's purpose. To be sure, the preacher can never force such growth in faith or faithfulness—that being affected by the workings of the Spirit and the exercise of free will—but the sermon can at least be designed and crafted with that ultimate intent.

NOTES

1. Zan Holmes, *Preaching Seminar, PR 80301*, Perkins School of Theology, Fall, 1983.
2. Barbara Brown Taylor, *The Preaching Life* (New York: A Crowley Publications Book, 1993), p. 84.
3. Charles L. Rice, *Preaching the Story* (Philadelphia: Fortress Press, 1980), p. 41.
4. Clyde E. Fant, *Preaching for Today* (New York: Harper and Row, 1975), p. 41.
5. H. Grady Davis, *Design for Preaching* (Philadelphia: Fortress Press, 1958), p. 288.
6. William H. Willimon, *Integrative Preaching* (Nashville: Abingdon, 1981), p. 27.
7. Fred B. Craddock, *As One without Authority* (Nashville: Abingdon, 1971), p. 41.
8. Henry H. Mitchell, *The Recovery of Preaching* (San Francisco: Harper and Row, 1977), p. 114.
9. Frederick Buechner, *Telling the Truth: The Gospel as Tragedy, Comedy and Fairy Tale* (New York: Harper and Row, 1977), p. 22.
10. Thomas G. Long, *The Witness of Preaching* (Louisville: Westminster John Knox Press, 2005), p. 3.
11. Mitchell, p. 12.

12. Lee and Kathryn Hayes Sparkes, ed., *Craddock on the Craft of Preaching* (St. Louis, Missouri: Chalice Press: 2011), p. 34.

13. Buechner, p. 36.

14. H. Grady Hardin, *"A Look in the Pulpit," Perkins Journal XXXVI* (Fall, 1982), p. 10.

15. Fred B. Craddock, *Overhearing the Gospel* (Nashville: Parthenon Press, 1978), p. 20.

16. H. H. Farmer, *The Servant of the Word* (Philadelphia: Fortress Press, 1942), p. 34.

CHAPTER TWO

TEN KEYS TO VITAL PREACHING

To this point I have focused on the issue of "What is preaching?" Now I turn to a different question: "What are keys to vital preaching?" I am hardly the first to construct a list of keys for effective preaching. Fred Craddock lists six "qualities" that should be pursued in preaching: "unity, memory, recognition, identification, anticipation, and intimacy."[1] Adam Hamilton mentions first the obvious requirements: that the sermon be "biblical, purposeful, adequately prepared, and emerging from prayer." Then he lists three keys to sermon impact: that the sermon is "*interesting, relevant* to the hearers' lives, and preached with genuine *passion*." [2] Certainly these are all important ingredients to vital preaching and my own list contains many of these same qualities. I choose, however, to put different labels on them and to add to the mix a few of my own. My "*keys to vital preaching*" take on the following headings:

Openness to the Spirit
Biblically Grounded
Theologically Sound
Identification
Connection
Dynamic Form
Being Oneself and More
Clarity of Focus
Passion
Purpose

These vital keys to preaching are not just an ambitious wish list. They are all essential to effective modern-day preaching. In an age of visual entertainment, competing values, and short attention spans, the preacher needs to be hitting on all cylinders in order to carry the message to its destination.

Unfortunately, all of these keys were not apparent to me as I began my preaching journey. They have evolved over the course of my entire ministry, some from study and seminars, others from the actual discipline of preaching week after week. Some I have always acknowledged: openness to the Spirit, biblical grounding, sound theology, and clarity of focus. Other dynamics became apparent only after years of preaching—such as utilizing the unique strengths and personality of the preacher, the importance of dynamic form, the huge benefit of long-range planning, and the daring but effective practice of preaching without notes. What has also changed over time is the relative value of each of these components. I now place a much higher value on what I call *identification* and *connection* which powerfully link the listener to the message and the messenger respectively. Such *connection* between the one who speaks and the one who hears is absolutely crucial in communication of all kinds, and certainly no less for the preaching experience.

Though these keys are not of equal importance, they are all valuable tools. Some elements are absolutely essential. Other elements relate to style or technique so that their relative importance depends in part upon the unique gifts and personality of the preacher. Whatever list of keys one might select as a preaching template—Craddock's six, Hamilton's combined seven, the ten I will share below, or one's own combination, they will undoubtedly bear testimony that good content is hardly all that is required of good preaching. If the method of conveying that content does not grab and hold the attention of today's listener, the sermon's message has little chance of being heard, much less heeded.

Effective preaching is not an ability to do one thing well but many things. These "ten keys to vital preaching" often make the difference between a good sermon and a poor one, an excellent sermon and one cloaked in mediocrity.

TEN KEYS: A CLOSER LOOK

1. OPENNESS TO THE SPIRIT

The first key to vital preaching is an openness to God's Spirit. This welcoming posture acknowledges the crucial partnership between the preacher and the Source of all Revelation. Such openness begins with a prayerful wrestling with the biblical text and continues throughout the preparation process. It recognizes that the content of the sermon is both "gift" and "art," that its creation has both a human and divine element. Openness to the Spirit does not end with preparation but continues to play a formative role even at the point of delivery. Many a preacher invites the Spirit into the time of proclamation by offering a familiar prayer: "Let the words of my mouth and the meditations of my heart, be acceptable to you, O Lord, my rock and my redeemer" (Psalm 19:14). Indeed, every preacher may be reassured that the Spirit will work in the hearts and minds of the congregation either through the power of the message, or at times, even in spite of it.

In his book, *The Witness of Preaching*, Thomas Long shares Theresa Rickard's analogy between the preaching act and the role of the midwife. Rickard describes that sacred task of birthing:

(The midwife)…has to be comfortable in the labor room; she is skilled and compassionate in bringing forth of life. The midwife does not create the child; the child has already been formed. The babies she delivers are not her possession, but a gift that she hands over. The midwife listens attentively to the heartbeat of both the mother and child… The new mother has the opportunity and responsibility to embrace and nurture her gift.[3]

Indeed, the preacher's role is not to create out of nothing, but begins with the text itself. With that text comes Jesus' promise: "But the Advocate, the Holy Spirit, whom the Father will send in my name, will teach you everything and remind you of all I have said to you" (John 14:26). In preaching, God's revelation passes through our hands, takes on our fingerprints, all the while remaining dependent upon the inspiration of the Spirit, and upon those who will receive and nurture that revelation into thought and deed. In the poignant time of sharing the message, we preachers should remember that though we have eye contact with the listener, we might also venture a glance upward, for the God for whom we speak, waits patiently to hear.

2. BIBLICALLY GROUNDED

Another essential key to vital preaching is that it be grounded in the Bible. This grounding actually begins in the preparation of the sermon by not only "listening" to Scripture, but also being personally addressed by it. This attention to Scripture requires that the central message of the sermon either emanate directly from the text(s) or find confirmation from the biblical message as a whole. If the sermon process has begun by addressing a human need or existential question, then the biblical grounding may well come from a variety of texts. If so, the preacher must be open to the message of these passages rather than simply using them to provide a biblical footnote to the preacher's own bias.

Since the rise to prominence of the narrative sermon in the past several decades, some have labeled such preaching as lacking in "biblical grounding." That comment sometimes comes from those who narrowly define a sermon as straight interpretation of a text with no appropriation for this time and place. It may also be a criticism from those accustomed to hearing a sermon with countless biblical quotes that punctuate the message. Thomas Long in *The Witness of Preaching* rightly understands that *biblical usage* does not mean *biblical preaching*. He draws a careful distinction:

> Biblical preaching has almost nothing to do with how many times the Bible is quoted in a sermon and everything to do with how faithfully the Bible is interpreted in relation to contemporary experience. "A sermon that begins in the Bible and ends in the bible," Edmund Steimle once observed, is not necessarily a biblical sermon." [4]

Even so, the criticism leveled against narrative preaching—that it sometimes lacks biblical grounding—may have some merit. Sometimes, the listener may not be able to discern a biblical connection to the message because the sermon, in its rush to be relevant, has failed to suggest any link with the biblical faith. It is important, even in the most creative preaching, that the narrative message point back to its scriptural source. This practice will not only increase the credibility of the preached word; it will also enhance the biblical and theological understanding of the laity.

A sermon is not required to be germinated directly from a text to be "biblically grounded." A sermon theme may properly find its origin in a human need or an existential dilemma. Even so, care must be taken to seek and find biblical support, allowing the text to speak for itself and not simply be used to support a position already determined. Through the careful work of exegesis the text can speak a new word to us, one we did not expect to find. Hardin heartily agrees. He concludes, "Sermon germs can come from anywhere, but they are not sermons until they have been nurtured in the Bible."[5] A sermon idea sprouting from the midst of life has the advantage of being relevant and current. However, if it is to have a chance of surviving as an authentic word, it must find root in the fertile soil of the biblical faith.

3. THEOLOGICALLY SOUND

Earlier I shared my notion that the preacher is the "resident theologian" of the church—not its only theologian—but one who has been given both authority and responsibility in that endeavor. Thus the sermon should always be tested for theological soundness. Two questions might be posed of every sermon: "Is the sermon's thesis grounded in the biblical faith?" or "Is the theology of the sermon merely a reflection of today's culture?" If these two questions had been raised and given proper deliberation, "success theology" would never have made it to even one Christian pulpit.

Even with the ability to pronounce some theologies as unfounded, unbiblical, or false, it is still difficult to define a "sound" theology. A preacher's first temptation is to assert that any theology is "sound" if it agrees with his or her own theology. A far more important point of agreement is with the Bible itself. For a sermon to have a sound theology there must be a consistency between the message and the biblical text. An additional concurrence is also required—that the theology expressed in the sermon is congruent with life experience. To be grounded in both Scripture and the human experience does

24

not dictate a specific theological position; but it does define one of the most important ground rules.

The goal of the sermon should not be simply to make a case for the preacher's own theology. The ultimate goal should be the theological prowess of the person in the pew. To that end the sermon should be more *open* than *closed* in order to allow for reflection and discernment by the listener. It is dialogue that often brings about change and maturation, not monologue. One must be careful, however, not to confuse theological openness with theological obscurity or indifference. The sermon should always reflect a sound theological position—one reached only after personal wrestling and offered more as a strong witness than as a decree from on high.

For the sermon to mirror a solid theology, it must also build on the integrity of the preacher. A willingness by the preacher to express at times confusion or theological wrestling will give a clear message to the hearer that theology is not something one discovers in a complete, ready-made form. Rather, it is painstakingly carved out of chunks of biblical thought and life experiences using a laser of spiritual insight and the chisel of the intellect. The path to a sound theology is one that always remains open to new growth and new insight. Our God may indeed be unchanging, but our understanding of God must be ever evolving if we are to come closer to the essence of God's nature and purpose.

4. IDENTIFICATION

Identification is not a new goal for effective preaching. The use of the parable in both the Old and New Testaments serves as a strong argument for the dynamic of *identification* in today's preaching. In fact, a parable's power comes most often from the listener *identifying* with the story. The climax of the parable may even take place internally as the listener is convicted by the parable's conclusion. At other times the connection is prompted by another. How well we remember the moment of truth when Nathan announces to David, "You are the man." (2 Samuel 12:7)

Jesus taught in parables using *identification* as its chief dynamic. His audience could first identify with the familiar life story (a farmer sowing seeds, a landowner seeking workers, a prodigal wanting his own way, a loving father welcoming a wayward son home). However, the true power of the parable's impact often came not from recognizing a familiar image, but rather by identifying with a person within the story (the prodigal, the jealous brother, the loving father, the laborers who worked all day). Once inside the story, the listener is almost forced to hear the word addressed directly to them—"Son, you are always with me and all that is mine is yours. But we had to celebrate and rejoice, because this brother of yours was dead and has come to life; he was lost and has been found." (Luke 15:31-32) "Take what belongs to you and go; I choose to give to this last the same as I give to you. Am I not allowed to do what I choose with what belongs to me? Or are you envious because I am generous?" (Matthew 20:14-15)

For today's sermon to be effective, the listener must find several points of *identification* within the message. At times, the point of identification may come straight from the text. As Paul writes to the church at Rome "For I do not do the good I want, but the evil I do not want is what I do..." (Romans 7:19) the hearers are "hooked" because they can identify with the text. Paul's words could easily have been *their* words. At other times, the point of *identification* comes with the preacher raising a bewildering existential question: "Why do bad things happen to good people?" All those who have experienced tragic loss are now fully engaged and ready to listen intently. They wonder, *"Will the preacher help me with this age-old question?"*

Another way the listener may *identify* with the sermon is through the preacher's use of real-life images rather than abstract thought. Jesus certainly was a master of this technique. He spoke of the familiar: a search for a lost coin, a time of harvest, the images of shepherds and sheep. He used metaphors of salt and light and bread. He also embellished concrete images by giving them an imaginative twist: "fishers of men" (Matthew 4:19) or "a camel passing through the eye of a needle" (Matthew 19:24) Such household word pictures helped to forge a connection between the "truth" Jesus proclaimed and the everyday life of his listeners.

Specific life images are far more effective than their abstract counterparts. Abstractions have no taste, color, sound, or smell. They do not engage the memory or emotions. Reflect on the power of creative imagery as Buechner translates Jesus' own imaginative warning against the rich:

> It is harder for a rich person to enter Paradise than for a Mercedes to get through a revolving door . . . , than for Nelson Rockefeller to get through the night deposit slot of the First National City Bank.[6]

Today's preacher remains tempted to speak in the abstract despite its ineffectiveness. It is easier to talk about love, forgiveness, and reconciliation than to provide these subjects with flesh and blood and place them in our immediate surroundings. Craddock wisely reminds us that *identification* is prompted by the *specific*, not by the *general* variety. Such application is preferable both for the ancient text and the modern day context.

> This means, then, that the sermon grows out of the dialogue between a particular passage (not a general and meaningless reference to what 'the Bible says') and a particular

congregation (not 'human situation'). What comes to fruition is not just a truth but the truth for this community.[7]

A preacher speaking on the theme of patience may be tempted to talk vaguely about the quality of patience and then urge everyone to try harder. Would it not be far better to help the congregation first *identify* with the topic at hand? Perhaps a reminder of our common teleprompter experience would be in order.

> "For English, press one. To hear a plug for new products, press two. To learn about our award-winning customer service, press three. To go to the main menu, press nine. To hear these options again press five. Thank you for your patience! Your time is so very, very important to us. A representative will be with you shortly." (Or maybe not!)

A preacher might be smart to discard the abstract jargon and simply begin with the human experience! Why not start by inviting the listener experience the "real world of impatience" before speaking of patience—a most elusive fruit of the spirit?

At times the main point of the sermon can be carefully hung on a word picture or retained in the mind by a life occurrence. If so, the *identification* can have staying power. Dr. Clay Oliphint in sermons delivered at First United Methodist Church of Richardson, Texas, provides us with examples of both. In one sermon he tells a story of a child at vacation Bible school who was asked what he had learned that week. They studied many biblical stories including the story of the risen Lord's encounter with two disciples on the road to Emmaus (Luke 24:13-34). One child thrust up his hand quickly. "I liked the "*Road to Amazing!*" This poignant phrase became the mantra for the sermon on All Saints Day. It was not used for cuteness or comic relief but as an imaginative and joyful refrain in the midst of a service comingled with both grief and hope. That imaginative and positive phrase proclaimed both the mystery and the power of resurrection; it made the sermon portable and accessible.

Likewise, in another sermon Oliphint drew from the cultural practice of "trick or treat" to speak of different responses to our receiving of gifts. The image was further empowered by the preacher acting out the exchange—the holding of the sack, the urging of parents to say the "magic words," the variety of responses to the gift of "treats." How easy it was to draw comparisons to how we, the listener, respond to the gifts God drops into our bag of blessings. In both sermons, the use of an image or imaginative phrase provided both movement and life to the message. It coaxed us into *identifying* with both the story and the message.

Perhaps the sermon should not be an invitation for the parishioner to enter into the world of the preacher, but rather an invitation for the preacher to enter the world of the parishioner. If so, the success of *"identification"* will depend mainly on how well the preacher understands the members and the daily images that surround them. Before the listener can "identify" with the sermon, the preacher must first "identify" with them and the world in which they reside.

5. CONNECTION

If *identification* is the important link between the listener and the message, *connection* is the crucial tie between the listener and the preacher. This connection may well be experienced as a personal one. It is dependent on a variety of factors.

One of my strong convictions about preaching, especially in today's culture, is that the listener not only wants to hear a great sermon; the listener wants to experience a "real person." In an address to the senior class at Divinity College,

Cambridge, Ralph Waldo Emerson spoke these words about a preacher who failed to exhibit such humanity.

> I once heard of a preacher who sorely tempted me to say I would go to church no more . . . A real snowstorm was falling around us. The snowstorm was real, the preacher merely spectral, and the eye felt the sad contrast in looking at him, and then out of the window behind him into the beautiful meteor of the snow. He had lived in vain. He had no word intimating that he laughed or wept, was married or in love, had been commended or cheated or chagrined. If he had ever lived and acted, we were none the wiser for it.[8]

The congregation wants to be convinced that the person who stands before them is an authentic human being. They want to see a part of the messenger disclosed as they receive the message itself. For the congregation to believe that The Story is "their story," it is important that they first hear the message as the "preacher's story."

Not long ago a friend of mine was coming as a guest preacher to my church. I wanted him to do a great job. He did. One reason he succeeded was that he came across as a caring, funny, likable guy—all words I would use to describe him. Had he tried to come across as intellectual, reserved, and polished I'm not sure his sermon would have been as well-received. That day he made a real *connection* with the people gathered for worship. Why? How? Simply put: the right person showed up.

Another factor in whether or not a strong *connection* is made between the congregation and the preacher is the delivery itself. I am not talking here about hand gestures, or eye contact per se. I am speaking of the delivery as "preaching presence." Such "presence" is affected greatly by how the preacher uses manuscripts and notes as aids to memory. Permit me to highlight my own journey toward "preaching presence."

Looking back on my ministry I had three delivery stages: (1) preaching from extensive notes after doing a rough draft manuscript, (2) preaching from a "polished" manuscript trying to look down as little as possible, and (3) preaching without notes (with a half sheet outline in my Bible for emergency use only). In each stage the quality of the content was much the same. The preparation time was also similar in length though very different in process. The results were not equal, however. I can say with absolute certainty that my preaching without notes has been by far the most effective method and preaching from a manuscript definitely the least effective.

One danger of committing to a polished manuscript is that it can easily become more "literary" than "oral." Sentences become longer and more complex. The more polishing one does, the greater the commitment to saying the words exactly as they are written and thus the greater temptation to look down at the manuscript to get the sentence exactly right. During my "manuscript period" copies of my sermons were mailed to people around the country and were often well received. Regrettably, sermons during this period were far better "read" than "heard."

Preaching today, if it is to be effective, must create a *connection* between the preacher and the person in the pew. A "conversational style" can be a most effective means of creating that *connection*. This style is quite different from a "top down" lecture style of preaching. By "conversational" I do not mean folksy, off-the-cuff or devoid of intimacy and intensity. Conversational preaching is not akin to greeting someone casually, engaging in small talk all the while looking over the shoulder for the next person in the room to visit. Rather, it is the kind of presence that is authentic, engaged, and truly present to the other. John Wesley had a term that conveys both the connection and its intimacy. He encouraged preachers to have "holy conversations." Perhaps that would be a good term for the exchange between the preacher and the congregation—a "holy conversation"—involving at the same time the authentic presence of a preacher and that of a caring pastor.

I certainly know first-hand that when a preacher pays too much attention to a manuscript, it can undermine the message. I once heard a preacher say with great passion: "I will never forget what my father told me," only to immediately look down at her notes. I wanted to shout out to her: "If your father's words are really something you will never forget, then why do you need to look down?" I am sure her downward glance was simply a nervous habit and not an effort to retrieve those memorable words, but her glance away from us made the words of her father less believable and the poignancy of the moment was lost. Perhaps an analogy might help: "A preacher constantly bobbing up and down looking at notes is like a dog lapping up water with an occasional look upward to convince his owner that he really cares more about him than the contents of the bowl." [9]

I must be quick to point out that the narrative style I am presently promoting is not manuscript memorization—reciting what has been written. Nor is it an act of "improv" in sharing the word. The "oral" style requires that the general content has been carefully memorized not as a precise script but more like a sequence of stories. The plot is all there and so are the important turn of phrases and images, but there is always room for an ad lib—sometimes from the playfulness of the preacher's personality and sometimes from the prompting of the Holy Spirit. Throughout my ministry I have always believed that many of my sermon "insights" were more gifts of the Spirit than the creations of my own imagination. In the scary business of preaching without notes (or "preaching without a net") one may well discover that the same Spirit that can speak to us in the study can also speak "live" in the very midst of the preaching moment.

My preaching without notes has indeed fostered a closer connection with the worshipper whether that gathering is composed of my own parishioners or that of relative strangers joined together only by our common faith. Such preaching, often standing outside the pulpit, has the feeling of being more vulnerable than when nestled behind the fortress of the pulpit and amply armed with a well-polished document. The result of preaching without notes with all its vulnerability is a more human persona. Freed from my notes, I can now respond to those who listen, using eye contact not as a means of trying to project sincerity, but as a way of reading how they are hearing the message. Such facial feedback may mean I cut a story short as I see quick recognition or continue my thought further until puzzled expressions finally resolve into signs of comprehension.

6. DYNAMIC FORM

Perhaps the most important lesson I have discovered about preaching is the critical importance of sermon form. Dr. Fred Craddock is credited more than any other for freeing us from the boring form of rational discourse, the template for the deductive sermon.[10] Craddock suggests that the preacher invite the listener into the journey of discernment rather than offering a festive package complete with a card that reads: "Here is the answer!" Craddock rightly understands that the effectiveness of the sermon depends as much on form as it does on content. Even though one could argue that the content itself is of greater value than the method that presents it, without an effective "delivery system" the content will seldom be heard.

In chapter eight of *Preaching*, Craddock comes finally to ask, "What form will the sermon take?" Craddock insists this is a crucial question. He argues his case for its importance:

> Arriving at something to say and crafting that message into a sermon are two separate processes with quite different demands and dynamics. Our efforts thus far have been in pursuit of the message itself. Before us now is the task of shaping and designing that message in order that it may be heard and appropriated. Here all the person's art and skill as a communicator join his or her care and understanding as minister in the creation of the sermon. That the preacher has a message does not mean that the listeners will get the message.[11]

What this change of form has meant in the field of preaching is a departure from simply telling listeners what they need to know and opting instead for the listener to be a part of the conversation. Consider the "top down" mantra of the old didactic form: "Tell them what you are going to tell them; tell them; and then tell them what you told them." Does this sound exciting? The difference between the new version of sermon shape and the old one is like comparing a sumptuous feast to a nutritious shake. In the first model, the newer one, the listener is invited to a gourmet feast where everyone may savor each bite, drink in the sights and sounds and join in delightful company. The listeners are a part of the feast and are treated as welcomed guests. In the other model, the older one, the same delectable meal is prepared, but instead of arranging the tasty morsels artistically on the plate and bringing it in person to the table, it is dumped into the blender, pureed into a green liquid and served up in a shiny plastic cup. The contents of both meals have the same nutritional value but in the old model all the chewing, savoring, and anticipating has been done ahead of time. The only job left for the listener is to swallow it! One can hardly wait!

Craddock suggests that the old didactic style provides no anticipation and is often devoid of imagination. He insists that this style of preaching would be like going to a child at bedtime and saying, "Well, I don't have time for the whole story but I want to give you basically the gist of it in three points." Such an approach is ineffective. Rather than *make points*, Craddock suggests that we help the listener *experience* the point. [12]

No one in this new paradigm would suggest that there is one form above all others—quite the contrary. A variety of forms is quite useful and follows the example of biblical texts themselves. Consider the radical changes in the biblical message if every book, indeed every major passage of the Bible, were forced into the mold of one form. The richness of the biblical story would be compromised and the content would be in danger as well. The prologue to John would not be as effective as a parable. The parable of the Laborers in the Vineyard would lose all of its punch if it were told as a metaphor or as history.

Craddock assists those of us who have little imagination to create new forms. He offers for us some examples of classic forms ready for our use:

- What is it? What is it worth? How does one get it?
- Explore, explain, apply
- The problem is, the solution
- What it is not, What it is
- Either/ or
- Both/ and
- Promise/ fulfillment
- Ambiguity, clarity
- Major premise, minor premise, conclusion
- Not this, nor this, nor this, nor this but this
- The flashback (from present to past to present)
- From the lesser, to the greater [13]

It was in my reading for my D. Min. in preaching that I first began to question the old model of sermon organization.

Mitchell, in his book, *The Recovery of Preaching*, suggested that most White Protestants organized their sermons in a very rational structure.[14] I began to realize that Mitchell had described the form of most of my sermons—held together by the logical structure of points and sub-points. I tried to reassure myself that I had good transitions and my sermons "held together."

Eugene Lowry in an article entitled "The Revolution of Sermonic Shape" joins Mitchell's critique of rational structure. He contrasts succinctly the difference between the old didactic form and the new one advocated by Craddock and others, including himself. Lowry recites the difference:

> A paradigm shift from deductive to inductive, from rhetoric to poetic. . .from literality to orality…from science to art, from left brain to right brain, from proposition to parable, from direct to indirect, from construction to development, from description to image, from authoritarian to democratic, from truth to meaning, from account to experience. [15]

As I read Craddock and Lowry and experienced firsthand their compelling preaching styles, I became convinced that sermon form needed more drama and suspense, creating anticipation in the listener. I began to envision a sermon form, not in terms of a logical outline, but now as "dramatic movement."

During one of my preaching classes I heard a sermon that followed a rational, deductive outline. When the time came for feedback, I was critical of the form used even though I recognized that it was painfully close to my dominant style. As the semester progressed, I developed a strong preference for sermons with creative form and grew increasingly dissatisfied with those held together by a rational framework. I found myself strongly favoring "dramatic movement" over "logical structure" or "rational discourse."

The final confirmation of my new preference came when I decided to rewrite an old sermon and put it into a more narrative style, one with movement and anticipation. I saved the main thrust of the sermon for last instead of presenting it at the first and following it with further development. I built suspense into the movement of the revised sermon. When I shared my "new" sermon with my wife, she was very enthusiastic—much more than usual. Surprisingly, she did not realize she had heard almost all the content before in a previous sermon. Just for fun, I pulled out the manuscript of the original sermon and began to read it to her. She was quickly bored, even though the content was basically the same. To my embarrassment, I had to force myself to finish it, having become bored myself with the reading of it. When I finally uttered the last word of the sermon, my wife and I bent over to take the sermon's pulse. Sure enough, it was already dead. The next day we held a simple graveside service!

In his classic book, *The Homiletical Plot*, Lowry has many helpful suggestions for those who desire more dramatic flair for their sermons. He prefers the term "movement or plot" over "outline."[16] His idea is to begin the sermon with an ambiguity. The sermon becomes an unfolding of how that ambiguity is resolved. The message climaxes with a reversal and a resounding "aha"!

Craddock adds to Lowry's method similar insights. His advice to young preachers is "Build the nest before you lay the egg."[17] He also speaks a word about movement: "Perhaps it will not be taken as irreverent to say that the movement of a sermon is as the movement of a good story or a good joke."[18] After all, who would begin a joke with the punch line or give the last page as the beginning of the book?

It would be a prudent practice for preachers to spend less time searching for the perfect illustration and more time discerning an appropriate form for the sermon. Don't ever declare that form is unimportant. It is the vehicle that delivers the goods!

7. BEING ONESELF AND MORE

I am convinced that every sermon should carry with it the preacher's fingerprints. Every sermon should have some sign of the unique talents or personality of the preacher. I first came to this conclusion at the mid-point of my preaching career. By then I had read scores of books on preaching. Few of them paid much attention to the uniqueness of the individual preacher. Style and technique seemed to be selected on the basis of their general effectiveness without much regard for the talent, inclination, or personality of the preacher. I began to realize that unless my unique gifts were used fully, my preaching would be less effective. Imagine the fate of Hebrew history had David chosen Saul's armor instead of his unorthodox sling!

Soon after formulating my thesis that every preacher needs to put his or her stamp upon a sermon, I discovered an article by Dr. Grady Hardin. It turns out my idea was not unique after all. Hardin writes:

> I want to affirm my high theology of the sermon, but I want to do it by reminding us of the Doctrine of Incarnation, too. It would have ruined the whole story if Moses had come down the hill pointing to the shine on his face. It would have been equally ineffective if he had backed down. The glory of God was seen in the face of Moses while he was being Moses.[19]

Besides my unique personality, I bring certain talents along with me as I prepare to enter the pulpit. The three special skills I carry in my gunny sack are the *use of words, creativity, and humor.*

My flair for *word usage* has proven helpful in the creation of catchy phrases that can be remembered, alliterations that capture the ear, and phrases and sentences that hopefully produce clarity of thought. Unfortunately, my word usage strength is often more dominant in the literary mode than in spoken or oral form. I have to be careful that my turn of phrase is not too complex or contrived. When used properly, wise word choice can be an aid to remembering, a handy "to-go box" to take home after the service.

Besides word usage my creativity is often utilized in using different forms and structures for my sermons. I certainly am not aware of a dominant or regular form for my preaching. I enjoy finding different means for holding a sermon together. Sometimes, I will use a gradual unfolding of an idea, almost like a journey. Occasionally, I will write a sermon completely in story form. I enjoy doing these the most but they also require the most time, creativity, and effort. At other times I use my creativity in writing an expansion of a parable. Creativity is my greatest friend in the endeavor of determining the form and shape of the sermon. It has helped me avoid boredom in the sermon process and I trust has at times prevented boredom in the pew as well.

One of the strengths of embodying one's unique qualities in preaching is that it is often experienced as an authentic sharing of one's self. A certain energy is released. Since music and humor are two of my talents, I once decided to engage both of them in an Advent sermon. I thought it would help me be more "present and real." I incorporated into the sermon a joke (not my usual practice) that related directly to the biblical text. The joke also made use of a clever pun—my favorite form of humor. My musical talent was utilized by including a hymn in the message. The words of the hymn interpreted well the meaning of the Scripture. Toward the end of the week I decided to sing the hymn a cappella rather than reading it aloud. It was a fitting conclusion to the sermon.

For the most part, both the joke and the solo were extremely well received. The congregation actually laughed out loud at the joke (a rarity for them). They were also unusually attentive during the singing of the hymn. Such sharing of my true self also had its risks. On one of the sermon evaluation forms (used as a part of my Doctor of Ministry Project) I received this impassioned plea concerning my future preaching: "Please, no more singing or corny jokes."

The sharing of one's talents in the pulpit has one obvious danger: egotism. Sharing one's talents must always be done as offering, not as glorification of the self. If humility becomes difficult, I would suggest soliciting numerous lay evaluations after each sermon. I am certain, no matter how good the sermon, someone will always be able to protest, "Please no more . . .!"

8. CLARITY OF FOCUS

One of the very few things I remember about my first seminary preaching class was the insistence that each sermon have a "sermon sentence"—a statement of the main point of the message. If I learned only this one lesson that semester, it was well worth the semester's tuition. A preacher's greatest curse may not be sharing too few thoughts but too many. Craddock says it best: "To say one thing each Sunday for fifty weeks is good medicine; to say fifty things each Sunday is to distribute aspirin in the waiting room."[20]

The importance of a clear focus for the sermon is obvious when it is not present. Too many ideas going in too many directions leave the person in the pew confused, if not frustrated. Even if the minister has many insightful things to say, if there is no unity of thought, no continuity of movement, then the sermon is not likely to have an impact on the listener, and little chance of being remembered past Sunday lunch. So, why not write a sermon sentence and avoid the confusion? If preachers do not know where they are going, it is unlikely the congregation will be able to make the journey.

Some might suggest that clarity of purpose is not so important when using narrative or inductive methods of preaching. I would argue just the opposite; these forms need clarity of purpose even more than deductive sermons. Telling stories and being in a conversational style can lead to too many asides and prolonged embellishment of details. It is best to have clarity of focus to add some direction and provide some parameters. Without such clarity of purpose the church hallways will be filled with one prevailing question: "What exactly was the preacher saying to us this morning?"

Clarity of focus should not be understood as meaning one thought or only a *singular* message. A sermon sentence, a good requirement of any sermon, can be a complex sentence in more ways than one. Take, for example, Jesus' message of the parable of the Prodigal son. The central message may point to the nature of God being like the unconditional love of the father in the story. Even so, there is also a message to the elder brother and to the prodigal himself. To have clarity of thought, one that can be stated in a simple sentence, will never limit the sermon to only one insight, but hopefully the hearer will not miss the main one!

Clarity of focus remains one of the most important disciplines of the sermon process. A preacher must learn to bite off and chew no more than the congregation can digest. Clarity of focus raises the odds that the message will be heard and quadruples the chances that the sermon will be remembered long enough to be put into practice.

9. PASSION

Adam Hamilton is his book on preaching lifts up passion as one of the three critical ingredients to effective preaching. He makes a personal appeal to preachers of the value of passion:

> When you are convinced that the word you are preaching is true, that it is an authentic word from the Lord, and when you have actually sought to live this word, or have seen it work in your life—and when you can get excited about this important word you have to share, others will sit up and take notice. [21]

Such passion occurs at several levels and in different points of the sermonizing process. First of all, it requires a personal involvement with the biblical text. If the preacher has a strong conviction of the truth of the text, that fervor will be apparent to the congregation. The first goal then is for the preacher to be personally involved in the message. The second goal is for that involvement to be "perceived" by the congregation. It is not enough to speak about God or to simply speak with enthusiasm. It is to be a first-hand account and a celebration worth sharing. Craddock invites us to share the Gospel with passion.

> Why not sermons that celebrate the unconditional love of God? Instead of using Thanksgiving to scold the ungrateful, why not a doxological message? Instead of the weary harangues against commercialism at Christmas and the

attacks against the once-a-year churchgoers at Easter, would it not be just as courageous to announce the Good News? Some Sunday mornings the minister should take the congregation by the hand and with them step off the dimensions of their inheritance as Children of God. Some of them have been "preached" at for years but have never been given a peek into the treasury, much less to run their fingers through the unsearchable riches of Christ. [22]

The congregation would like to know that a person of faith stands before them. They want to hear passion in the voice of the messenger as they receive the message. For the congregation to believe that The Story is "their story," they must first believe it is truly the "preacher's story."

10. PURPOSE

The last key to vital preaching is purpose, though chronologically it is first. Adam Hamilton reminds us that purpose is a part of the text itself and worthy of discernment at the time of exegesis. Certainly the biblical writers understood their particular purpose for their proclamation, whether it is explicitly stated or not. For example, the writer of John's Gospel reveals the purpose for his proclamation: "But these are written so that you may come to believe that Jesus is the Messiah, the Son of God, and that through believing you may have life in his name" (John 20:31). In like manner, we preachers, entrusted with sharing God's word, need to be aware of *our purpose* in preaching—not in some general or generic way but the specific purpose for each proclamation. We cannot control the listener's response (that being in God's hand), but we can control our intent—what we hope transpires in the lives of all those who hear.

VITAL PREACHING

Perhaps the preacher, in the process of preparing the sermon, should ask a simple question of the sermon: "So what?" What do I want the community of faith to do with this message? Do I intend a growth of faith, a movement toward confession, a rebirth of hope, a dismantling of prejudice, a discarding of resentment, an embrace of forgiveness? How tragic if the sermon asks nothing of the listener—no decision, no action implied or suggested! Sermons that matter, that make a difference in people's lives, will always have the pulse of purpose in their veins, inviting the hearer to see things from a different perspective, to embrace the good news, to find fitting work in God's service, and on the way to experience a renewed and compassionate spirit.

NOTES

1. Fred Craddock, *Preaching* (Nashville: Abingdon Press, 1985), p. 155.
2. Adam Hamilton, *Unleashing the Word* (Nashville: Abingdon Press, 2003), p. 37.
3. Thomas G. Long, *The Witness of Preaching* (Louisville: Westminster John Knox Press, 2005), p. 13.
4. Long, p. 52.
5. H. Grady Hardin, *"A Look in the Pulpit," Perkins Journal XXXVI* (Fall, 1982), p. 10.
6. Frederick Buechner, *Telling the Truth: the Gospel as Tragedy, Comedy, and Fairy Tale* (New York: Harper and Row, 1977), p. 22.
7. Fred B. Craddock, *As One without Authority* (Nashville: Abingdon, 1971), p. 130.
8. Charles L. Rice, *Preaching the Story* (Philadelphia: Fortress Press, 1980), p. 19.
9. Justin Tull, *Surviving and Thriving in Ministry* (2013), pp. 94-95.
10. Long, p. 102.
11. Craddock, *Preaching*, p. 153.
12. Lee and Kathryn Hayes Sparkes, ed., *Craddock on the Craft of Preaching* (St. Louis, Missouri: Chalice Press: 2011), p. 54.
13. Craddock, *Preaching*, p. 177.
14. Henry H. Mitchell, *The Recovery of Preaching* (San Francisco: Harper and Row 1977), p. 11.

15. Gail R. O'Day and Thomas G. Long, ed., *Listening to the Word* (Nashville: Abingdon Press, 1993), pp. 95-96.
16. Eugene L. Lowry, *The Homiletical Plot* (Atlanta: John Knox Press, 1980), p. 16.
17. Fred B. Craddock *Overhearing the Gospel* (Nashville: Parthenon Press, 1978), p. 5.
18. Craddock, *As One without Authority*, p. 62.
19. Hardin, p. 3.
20. Craddock, *As One without Authority*, p. 107.
21. Adam Hamilton, p.43.
22. Craddock, *As One without Authority*, p. 88.

CHAPTER THREE

WHAT TO PREACH

SELECTING THE TEXTS

One of the most important tasks preachers have is the selection of the text(s) for the sermon. The use of lectionary readings is a prudent way to begin the search for such texts. As I began my preaching ministry, I did not turn to the lectionary for possible texts but instead relied on my own biblical knowledge and favorite texts. After about half a year of selecting my own texts, my limited biblical sources were significantly depleted. In part out of necessity I began relying on the lectionary readings more and more as the source for my sermon text(s). I rarely preached the lectionary text on the corresponding Sunday, but at least I was broadening the biblical base of my preaching.

A CASE FOR THE LECTIONARY

Shelly E. Cochran, in an article on the lectionary, points to several advantages of preaching from this accepted source. Listed below are some of the benefits of using the lectionary including most of those she mentions in her article. [1]

Benefits:
- Expands the preacher's scope of the Bible
- Aids long-range planning
- Maintains unity with other churches
- Parallels Christian educational materials
- Invites the preacher to preach on difficult texts
- Provides access to many resources based on the lectionary

- Invites the preacher to preach from the Old Testament, the Psalms, and the Epistles instead of relying mainly on the Gospels.
- Follows the church year[1]

PUTTING THE LECTIONARY IN PERSPECTIVE

With all these benefits the lectionary still does not release the pastor from the ultimate responsibility of text selection. After I was ordained, my hands were placed on the Bible and the bishop spoke the words, "Take authority to preach the word…" Notice that the bishop did not say, "Take authority to preach the lectionary." Even so, some ministers have become totally committed to the lectionary as the sole source for preaching. They stay with the lectionary selections, Sunday after Sunday, regardless of what is happening in the church, the community or the world at large.

As I prepared for my D. Min project I had an opportunity to discuss my plans with Dr. Albert Outler, a revered professor at my seminary. After talking with him about my project, he asked me why I had decided to use the lectionary readings as the texts for my four Advent sermons. I told him, "So the selection of texts won't be arbitrary." Outler responded quickly and with a playful smile, "Justin, the lectionary itself is arbitrary." Outler had an astute point. Just because several well-informed, well-educated people decided on the most important texts and their proper order does not dictate that these texts should be mandatory for all preaching. The lectionary has weaknesses as well as strengths. Eugene Lowry in his book *Living with the Lectionary,* begins his discussion, not with the advantages of using the lectionary, but with its shortfalls. [2]

Limitations:

- Makes Old Testament and epistle texts subordinate to the Gospel selection
- Does not include the entire Bible and omits many significant passages.
- Often omits troublesome verses within the text
- Omits many texts about the women of the Bible
- Makes sermon series problematic
- Stresses thematic unity over diversity of thought within the Bible
- Provides a shortcut to further biblical research by use of prolific lectionary aids.

TIMES FOR DEPARTURE

Considering that the lectionary has both strengths and weaknesses, the pastor is left with the decision of how to use the lectionary, if at all. I would certainly argue that the lectionary texts be the first and main source for preaching texts. Even so, times will occur when the lectionary texts should not dictate the text for a particular Sunday. Listed below are just a few examples of when to deviate from the lectionary:

- The occurrence of significant national events
- When emphasizing a church-wide program
- In the midst of a serious church crisis
- When developing a sermon series

When a major tragedy occurs, that event needs to be addressed by the preacher. Sometimes, this issue can be mentioned in the service, including the time of prayer. Other times, the issue or crisis is serious enough to command the full time of the message. The event of 9/11, for example, called for a sermon that would wrestle with such injustice and atrocity. To be silent in the face of such a tragedy would suggest either that the event was not important enough to be addressed or that the biblical faith was not adequate enough to tackle such an event. A preacher is obligated to speak about issues that significantly impact the nation, the community, and the worshipping congregation.

When I was appointed to a church following the death of their senior pastor only four days before, I looked at the lectionary readings for that Sunday as I began my preparations to preach. I did not feel compelled, however, to use any of the texts. I eventually choose an Advent text though it was not the one designated for that Sunday. As the new "resident theologian" my responsibility was to choose an appropriate text for a hurting congregation while placing it within the context of the Advent season. During my remaining six months of that interim appointment, I ventured away from the lectionary texts most of the time, choosing instead texts that spoke to a church wrestling with grief and issues of faith. Later, as the congregation's grief subsided, I shifted the focus of the sermons. The timing of these sermon choices was as important as the message they conveyed. Had I simply "stuck to the lectionary," with its specific texts and its fixed schedule, I would have run the risk of ignoring the specific and timely needs of the people who would hear the message.

PREACHING IN ADVENT

Of all the lectionary readings, I have the most difficulty with those chosen for the first Sunday of Advent which concentrate on "the Last Days" motif in the Gospel selections and echoes the same theme in the Old Testament readings. The end of time is certainly a problematic theme worthy of exploration due to frequent misinterpretations by many of today's preachers. However, I find the foreboding character of the readings out of place in Advent even though it does contain the Advent theme of "waiting." In the lectionary Gospel readings (Matthew 24:36-

44, Mark 13: 24-37, and Luke 21:25-36), the waiting is not for "peace among those whom he favors" (Luke 2:14b) but for a day of future judgment. The last days would come about through intervention and power, while the birth of Christ would be marked by its astounding vulnerability. These two contrasting themes do not work well together.

On one occasion I preached in Advent on the "Faces of the Nativity." I began on the first Sunday in Advent not with texts on the "last days" but with Mary's story and continued on subsequent Sundays with the story of Joseph, followed by those of shepherds and wise men, and ending with the Christ child story on Christmas Eve. During other Advent seasons my sermons been careful to address the "problems" of the Christmas season for many—loss of loved ones, the pace of the season, a lack of hope, or disinterest in the ancient story. The preacher has a responsibility to help the congregation prepare for the good news of Jesus' birth. That certainly can be done with the lectionary texts, but it can also be done creatively using any of the texts that lead to the incarnation. The preacher needs to find a way to share an appropriate and powerful word concerning Jesus' birth with those in desperate need of the Christmas message.

PREACHING THE BIG PICTURE

One of the drawbacks to using lectionary texts exclusively is that its choices of Old Testament, Psalms, and Epistle readings are primarily to lend thematic support. This thematic approach stresses biblical consistency. However, the Bible also contains no small amount of biblical tension. Consider the book of Job and its argument against the biblical wisdom of its day. In using the lectionary texts, a preacher may be tempted to follow the lectionary's lead by always choosing texts that are in agreement with each other rather than wrestling with biblical complexity. If the congregation is to learn an overview of the Bible, the preacher must take the lead in showing how the various parts, some even seemingly contradictory, fit together. To help provide a biblical overview, the preacher may intentionally choose to use Scriptures in tension with each other. For example, a preacher could choose to preach using two texts—one from Matt.16: 24 "If any want to become my followers, let them deny themselves and take up their cross and follow me." The other text is from Matthew 11:28-30, "Come to me, all you that are weary and are carrying heavy burdens, and I will give you rest." These two passages seem at first to contradict each other—"Is the Christian life easy or difficult?" On closer examination these two texts reflect different aspects of the Christian life—both the sacrifice required of discipleship and the blessings yielded by such a life. The preacher is the one who can help offer the "big picture" of what it means to be a Christian—not a life of only sacrifice and not one of simply ease and comfort. Either by itself is a distortion. Taken together, they portray the life of the Christian.

The lectionary readings primarily avoid such biblical tension. By using a thematic approach of grouping like-minded texts, the preacher may fail to develop dialogue with other texts. In preaching on prayer, for example, it is not enough just to expound on the text, "Ask and it will be given you; search, and you will find; knock, and the door will be opened for you" (Matthew 7:7). The lectionary groupings give the preacher little help in finding texts that might challenge the "unconditional" nature of prayer. One text not even included in the lectionary might serve as a secondary text—James 4:3. Its words suggest that all requests are not granted. It reminds the reader that "you ask and do not receive, because you ask wrongly, in order to spend what you get on your pleasures."

Because of the lectionary's reliance on thematic unity, it is important that the preacher allow any text chosen to be in dialogue with the Bible as a whole. These "complimentary texts" may serve the preacher well as additional texts for the sermon rather than solely relying on the groupings selected by the lectionary. I wonder how different preaching from the lectionary would be if texts had been grouped by contrasting themes rather than those with similar thought. Had the lectionary scholars taken that radical approach, preaching those texts might be both more challenging for the preacher, and at times, perhaps more helpful to the listener.

MY USE OF THE LECTIONARY

In my first two-thirds of my ministry I preached primarily from the lectionary readings but rarely on the Sunday prescribed. In my last ten years of preaching, I relied much more on texts not listed in the lectionary. I also preached more series based on a block of scripture—for example, the "sermon on the mount" found in Matthew 5-7. The Gospel writer clearly grouped these sayings of Jesus into one block of teaching, yet the lectionary shares only bits and pieces of it often separating the various passages by eight or nine months. What Mathew chose as a block of Scripture, the lectionary has treated as individual passages to be scattered throughout the church year rather than placed in its original context. I preached a series of sermons on the "sermon on the mount" and found it helpful to do so in Matthew's original context.

Each preacher must decide what role the lectionary should play in text selection. My position is that the lectionary texts are a wonderful place to start but not worthy of totally determining the preacher's choice of texts or their designated times to be preached. To preach the word requires not only responsiveness to the biblical word but also a *reading* of the ones who would hear its message. The preacher's job is always to share an appropriate and timely word.

NOTES

1. David M. Greenhaw and Ronald J. Allen, ed., *Preaching in the Context of Worship* (St. Louis, Missouri: Chalice Press, 2000), pp. 63-64.
2. Eugene L. Lowry, *Living with the Lectionary* (Nashville: Abingdon Press, 1992), pp. 15-25.

CHAPTER FOUR

HOW TO PLAN LONG RANGE

LONG RANGE PLANNING

MY PLANNING JOURNEY

I have always believed in planning ahead. It is part of my nature. After I finish any meal, I am always planning the next one. Of course, in preaching one has to think a bit more long-term than that. By the time I was in my fourth church, I usually had about four sermons lined up at any one time. They were not fully developed—some had only a text, title and few main ideas. But at least I was not preparing sermons week to week.

I remember clearly when I changed my practice in sermon planning. I wish I could say it was at my initiative, but it was not. My new planning regimen came as a result of a request from my new music director: "I need your sermon plans for the next seven weeks." "Why seven weeks?" I asked. "Because I want to plan the anthems to fit the sermons and I need to work on them with the choir for about seven weeks. Can you get me your sermon texts and titles soon?" I can't remember how quickly I responded to her request but I know that before I left the church two years later, I had managed to complete three to four months of sermon plans at a time. [1]

Several years later I served a church that had no parsonage so my wife and I decided to build, a process that normally lasts six months to a year. We had a fantastic builder, however, and he built the house, a wonderful house, in only three months. How did he do it? He always tried to have five or six houses going at once but in different stages. When a framer finished with one house, he would move to the next. When the painters were through with one house, another one would be ready for them. The builder kept all his subs busy and he orchestrated the different stages of each house with great precision.

A year or so after having built my first house, I attended a preaching workshop on long-range planning. I was fascinated by the leader's analogy—building a house. I was already anticipating his argument. I have paraphrased his sales pitch below.

> To build a house takes time. You don't start one week and finish it by the end of the week. You build it in stages. Building a sermon works the same way. When you are doing the finishing touches on one sermon you should have the foundation ready for another. You move each sermon along until it is time to be delivered.

Eventually, I learned to plan a majority of the sermons for a whole year. One clear advantage was the incubation time for many of the sermons. Some sermons required time to be mulled over in my conscious and sub-conscious mind. Advanced planning allowed sermons to reach their maturity before they were preached. Fred Craddock would certainly agree with the importance of such "incubation."

> Sermons that grow and mature over a long period of time are usually superior homiletically, theologically, and biblically—as well as in case and freedom of delivery—to those "gotten up" just days or even hours prior to presentation. In addition, those who work with the minister planning the worship service are able to do just that, work with the minister, rather than having to wait for a phone call, hoping that the now revealed text and subject do not tear the worship service from top to bottom like the curtain of the temple.[2]

STEPS TO CONSIDER

Those beginning significant long-range planning for the first time may want to make a case to the church for time off to do so. What better way to underscore that preaching is both important and requires significant work in order to be effective? The benefits to such early work are immense.

- Facilitates worship planning and coordination of the service
- Allows for systematic plan for the church year
- Allows incubation time for better sermon development
- Enables the preacher to ensure a better balance of sermon themes

PLANNING ESSENTIALS

- A place apart
- Sufficient time 3-5 days
- Balance of rest, reading, exercise, meditation, and work
- Access to a computer and internet
- Secure someone to fill the pulpit for the Sunday following the retreat.

RETREAT SCHEDULE

Day One

Read all lectionary texts for at least half the year making notes in the margin of the lectionary workbook. (I use the *Music and Worship Planner* produced by Abingdon Press). On this first day I begin a schedule that I repeat each day. This includes:

- Time for meditation and prayer
- Cooking simple meals with little preparation time
- Exercise
- A nature walk twice a day
- TV for news only in morning and evening.
- Thirty minutes of reading

- Remainder of time (about six hours) is devoted directly to sermon planning

Day Two

I go through the notes in the margins of the lectionary workbook and look for connections with the congregation. I decide on my "first picks" of texts to be used during the year. Those that show greatest promise, I tentatively place on the calendar. I tend to place these top picks in the first two months if they seem to work there. These sermons will take less incubation time than many of the others. When I have finished with this tentative schedule, I try to categorize all the potential sermons using the following categories:

- Teaching
- Christian life
- Evangelistic
- Existential
- Holy Days
- Prophetic
- Social justice
- Theological
- Discipleship
- Worship

Day Three

The third day is primarily devoted to finalizing the scheduling process. I try to schedule the first two months and then look ahead toward the rest of the year. As a calendar template I list special days or emphases for the year. This helps me decide on appropriate sermon texts.

Special Days	Time often celebrated
• Covenant Sunday	January
• Reaffirmation of Baptism	January

- Scout Sunday   February
- Ash Wednesday   February
- Good Friday   March
- Palm/Passion Sunday   March/April
- Easter Sunday   March/April
- Mother's Day   May
- Father's Day   June
- July 4th Sunday   July
- Labor Day   September
- Promotion Sunday   September
- Children's Sabbath   October
- Laity Sunday   October
- Pledge Sunday   October
- All Saints Day   November
- Veteran's Day   November
- Thanksgiving Sunday   November
- Advent/Christmas   December

Day Four

I go back over the lectionary workbook looking for other texts and brainstorming further the texts I have already selected for possible use during the year. I read the remainder of the lectionary texts for the year (if time permits) following the same procedure as before. I look again at the first two months of sermon plans and jot down more ideas for these eight sermons, with special care for the first sermon which will be preached in eight days.

Finalizing the Year

In July—usually during my vacation but counted as study leave—I take two or three days repeating the same process as in the longer retreat. This planning session takes less time because I have fewer lectionary texts to read, less Sundays to schedule, and I already have a surplus of sermon possibilities, ones not yet scheduled. By the end of this planning process I try to finalize the preaching schedule through January of the next year. As always, these are only my tentative plans, and both texts and scheduling can change as the year progresses. The good news is that I have a plan, and I can evaluate its diversity and balance and make adjustments if need be.

HAMILTON'S MODELS

Adam Hamilton in his yearly planning has five over-arching purposes for preaching during the church year: *evangelism, discipleship, pastoral care, equipping and sending,* and *institutional development.* These become a major part of the preaching calendar. In January and February evangelism is the theme. During lent there is an emphasis on discipleship. Pastoral care is a major focus for preaching in May and June. Equipping and sending is concentrated in the months of September and October. Institutional development is a theme of November. Advent is left open. [3]

As you can see, Hamilton gives greater weight to the local church year than the liturgical year. He directs much of his preaching toward the life of the local church. For most of my ministry my preaching was directed primarily at the individual life rather than the church as the community of faith. If I were starting out as a young preacher, I would strive for a better balance of each—sermons directed toward the community of faith and sermons directed toward the individual Christian.

FINAL WORD ON PLANNING

My evolution in long-range sermon preparation was initiated by a well-trained musician committed to planning ahead to insure good music production. That early lesson was later expanded and endorsed by countless seminars, conferences, and finally confirmed by practical experience. I only wish I had begun the practice in my first church instead of my fourth. Doing such planning has allowed me to see the broad strokes of my preaching and to be able to discern if my year long plan lacks balance or coherence. I highly recommend long range planning to all ministers who preach on a regular basis.

NOTES

1. Justin W. Tull, *Surviving and Thriving in Ministry* (2013), pp. 90-92.
2. Fred B. Craddock, *Preaching* (Nashville: Abingdon Press, 1985), pp. 101-102.
3. Adam Hamilton, *Unleashing the Word* (Nashville: Abingdon Press, 2003), pp. 16, 25.

CHAPTER FIVE

THE WORK OF EXEGESIS

For the purposes of this book I will not endeavor to supply a complex exegesis process. Instead, I begin by sharing an exegetical model put forward by Thomas Long.

LONG'S MODEL FOR EXEGESIS

Outline of Brief Exegetical Method for Preaching

I. Getting the Text in View
   A. Select the text
   B. Reconsider where the text begins and ends
   C. Establish a reliable translation of the text.

II. Getting Introduced to the Text
   D. Read the text for basic understanding
   E. Place the text in its larger context

III. Attending to the Text
   F. Listen attentively to the text

IV. Testing What I Heard in the Text
   G. Explore the text historically
   H. Explore the literary character of the text
   I. Explore the text theologically
   J. Check the text in the commentaries

V. Moving toward the Sermon
   K. State the claim of the text upon the hearers (including the preacher) [1]

Long has provided us with a marvelous checklist. These steps need not take an inordinate amount of time, especially as one becomes a seasoned student of the Bible. Their complexity, however, does initiate a dialogue of the preacher with the text, a dialogue that hopefully will be continued in some way in the sermon's narrative.

TAYLOR'S APPROACH

One danger of following such a careful regimen is to falsely understand the process as mainly academic and somewhat detached. It is the voice of Barbara Brown Taylor that calls us into a more intimate journey with the text. Any preacher would gain from adopting her holistic "method" of exegesis, one that reveres not only the text but also the community of faith which the text will ultimately address.

> For me, to preach is first of all to immerse myself in the word of God, to look inside every sentence and underneath every phrase for the layers of meaning that have accumulated there over the centuries. It is to examine my own life and the life of the congregation with the same care, hunting the connections between the word on the page and the word at work in the world. It is to find my own words for bringing those connections to life, so that others can experience them for themselves. When that happens— when the act of preaching becomes a source of revelation for me as well as for those who listen to me—then the good news every sermon proclaims is that the God who acted is the God who acts, and that the Holy Spirit is alive and well in the world. [2]

In the spirit of Taylor's sharing of the sacramental nature of the preaching act, let me offer a simpler exegetical outline I have developed and used over the years.

MY MODEL FOR EXEGESIS

READ AND REFLECT

- In a prayerful attitude, read the text silently and then aloud receiving its word afresh.
- Underline or highlight key words in the lectionary workbook, making notes in the margin.
- Put an exclamation point in the margin of what you strongly believe and question marks next to parts of the text that are confusing or difficult to believe.

BRAINSTORM AND INTERACT

- Determine the theme or themes of the text.
- With no regard as to possible use in the sermon, write down any thoughts that occur to you.
- Ponder what the text might mean for you and members of your congregation.

QUESTION AND TEST

- Feel free to question whether you really believe the message of the text. Will the meek really inherit the earth? Do we receive if we ask?
- Continue applying the text to life today.

STUDY AND DECIPHER

- With the aid of secondary sources, address and test your understanding of the text.
- Research the historical background of the text.
- Be sure to look at what precedes and follows the text. Does that add clarity?
- Use Gospel Parallels or annotations in your Bible to check for other similar passages. Read various translations of the text.
- Seek other texts that seem to agree or disagree with the text.
- Decide what portion of the text will be the focus of the sermon. Put it in your own words.

Regardless of the exegetical method, it is important for the preacher to "do the homework." Before we can interpret the word for our own day, we must be able to discern its original context and intent.

NOTES

1. Thomas G. Long, *The Witness of Preaching* (Louisville: Westminster John Knox Press, 2005), p. 70.
2. Barbara Brown Taylor, *The Preaching Life* (New York: A Crowley Publications Book, 1993), p. 33.

CHAPTER SIX

FROM TEXT TO PLOT

Once the exegesis is completed, it is time to apply the meaning of the text to life today. I go through a process with the goal of making the message relevant to the listener. I begin by asking several questions:

How does the text hold up to life experience? Mine? Others?

- Who do I know who would have trouble believing this text?
- Does the "wisdom" of our culture agree or disagree with the text?

GATHER MATERIALS

A key step in crafting the sermon is to gather all the ideas and images that relate to the central message of the text. The operative word is "imagination." Those who no longer employ this aptitude need to rediscover it. Imagination is an indispensable tool in the craft of preaching.

The goal is to gather more material than can possibly be used. One scholar equated this "construction stage" as bringing to the work site all the building blocks and materials that might be needed, even before knowing what the finished project might require. Another important part of this method is to refrain from trying to use every idea available at the sermon construction site. Save some of the good material for future sermons!

CHOOSE COMPONENT PARTS

The next step is to begin the selection process, choosing those ideas to be included in the sermon and those to be placed on temporary hold. One can select component parts from a variety of options such as, insights from the text, life stories, poignant and relevant illustrations, key phrases, and other biblical accounts. One might even create a story or analogy of one's own. After gathering the "first picks" of component parts, look at the grouping and ask some important questions:

- Are these components varied in type and in emotional intensity?
- Are they all relevant to the congregation?
- Are they believable?
- Which ones work best?
- Which ones would make a powerful ending or captivating beginning?

DECIDE ON DIRECTION AND PURPOSE

Before assembling the component parts of the sermon it is appropriate to ask questions and claim a direction.

- What is the purpose of this sermon? Write it in a sentence.
- What do you want to happen in the mind and heart of the listener?
- Do you intend that the listener make any decision? (discipleship, life stance, self perception, commitment)
- Do you hope for any action by the hearer?
- Do you seek the community of faith to make a change?
- With the sermon's purpose and intent clearly in mind, write a sermon sentence that captures the thrust of the sermon.

CHOOSE FORM AND SEQUENCE

Having the direction of the sermon and most of the component parts, begin to explore various possibilities for the form of the sermon. (See chapter two for examples.) Pay attention first to the form of the text to see if it conjures up a possible form for the sermon. After choosing the form, arrange the sequences of the sermon plot and then follow the steps below.

- Does the sermon create a sense of anticipation or is the theme given away too early?
- Do the parts fit together?

- Choose the beginning and ending.
- Does the plot of the sermon hold together? Anything to add? Take away?
- Finalize the sequence.

WRITE MANUSCRIPT

After deciding on sermon form and sequence, write a rough draft. Read it out loud. As you read, ask the following questions:

- Does this sound like an essay or a conversation?
- Is the style literary or oral?
- Am I excited about what I am saying?

PRACTICE SERMON WITHOUT MANUSCRIPT

Make notes of the main points of the manuscript using no more than 15 sequences. After carefully studying the new outline, try to give the sermon using the only the outline as a prompter. Now try to give the sermon without using either the manuscript or the outline. Make observations about how the sermon worked or did not work.

- What did you forget without the outline?
- What transitions did not work?
- What will give the sermon better continuity or more dramatic movement?
- Does the sequencing need to be changed?
- Revise the outline and then use it to give the sermon again.

FINE TUNE THE MATERIAL

Make any final adjustments to the sermon.

- Finalize exact wording for key phrases.
- Carefully script the last few sentences of the ending, including the last words.
- Practice the beginning. What are the first words to be spoken?

PREPARE FINAL NOTES OR MANUSCRIPT

Prepare the notes that you will be using in the service. If you will be using a manuscript, I advise an "abridged version," one with no illustrations or stories written out. A heading is often sufficient: "childhood Christmas memory" "story of distraught church member," "Lincoln's joke to his staff." Without a text available, the preacher will not be tempted to look down at the manuscript. With a note card outline or abridged manuscript in hand, the preacher must now prepare for the sermon's artful delivery.

CHAPTER SEVEN

PREPARING TO DELIVER

PLEA FOR PREACHING WITHOUT NOTES

Before looking at the steps required for an effective delivery, I must pause and make a final case for preaching without notes. This method is one of the most effective ways to make a "connection" with the listener. This method should not be confused with "extemporaneous," "off the cuff," or "shooting from the hip"—all which suggest little or no preparation. Preaching without notes, if it is to be done effectively, must be carefully scripted in order to avoid rambling, lack of focus, and clumsy endings. I find that preaching without notes takes about the same amount of preparation time as preparing a manuscript and then being able to deliver it with minimal dependence on the written document. However, the effectiveness of the two methods is markedly different.

Joseph M. Webb's book, *Preaching without Notes*, provides a step-by-step guide for mastering this method of delivery. Webb also offers a strong case *against* a "literary" manuscript style and a convincing argument *for* an "oral style." Webb begins by sharing a quote from John Broadus' book, *A Treatise on the Preparation and Delivery of Sermons*. His argument reveals the limitations of a literary style:

> As to delivery itself, reading is of necessity less effective, and in most cases immensely less effective, for all the great purposes of oratory, than speaking. Greater coldness of manner is almost inevitable. If one attempts to be very animated or pathetic, it will look unnatural. The tones of voice are monotonous, or have a forced variety. The gestures are almost always unnatural, because it is not

natural to gesticulate much in reading, and they scarcely ever raise us higher than to feel that really this man (or woman) reads almost like speaking. [1]

Later, Webb shares Broadus' convincing affirmation of the "oral style" over a "textual style."

As to the delivery itself, it is only in extemporaneous speaking, of one or another variety, that (the sermon) can ever be perfectly natural, and achieve the highest effect. The ideal of speaking, it has been justly said, cannot be reached in any other way. Only thus will the voice, the action, the eye, be just what nature dictates, and attain their full power. And while painstaking culture vainly strives to read or recite precisely like speaking, the extemporaneous speaker may with comparative ease rise to the best delivery of which he (or she) is capable. [2]

Please note that Broadus is not using "extemporaneous speaking" as meaning no preparation but in contrast to memorizing a written text. He is proposing a "conversational" tone and style, one I heartily endorse as well.

A Word of Warning

The preacher should not be seduced into believing that "oral style" can ever *save* a sermon with poor content. It cannot. Many years ago, I listened to a sermon tape of a candidate for ministry. It was a horrible sermon, lacking substance and biblical grounding. When I offered my negative assessment of his sermon, he insisted that the tape could not do justice to his preaching. He pleaded his case: "You just had to see me!" I was not convinced. No dancing or hand gestures or eye contact could have redeemed that sermon. Style, as important as it is, cannot be substituted for substance. Both are needed!

Thomas Long must have a similar opinion of the importance and limitations of human effort in preaching. He writes:

> Preaching is not a "science," of course, and almost every experienced preacher can report occasions when she or he was "in the zone," when the preacher rode the crest of the Spirit's wave and proclaimed a Word well beyond that which could be accounted for by wit and skill. The temptation inherent in such experiences, though, is to make them definitive of practice, to allow them to encourage haphazard preparation and inattention to the fine detail of excellence in the pulpit. It is one thing for preachers who have rigorously studied biblical texts, carefully honed the words and shapes of their sermons, and given thoughtful attention to body and gesture to find themselves exhilarated and humbled by becoming vessels of a Word beyond their mere human limitations. It is quite another for them to wander around the chancel with a wireless mike, a cheerful personality, and a thimble full of advance thought, holding their finger in the air and praying for lightning to strike. [3]

TESTING THE WATER

The change from using a manuscript to requiring no notes at all is a scary and initially precarious endeavor. I made my first major transition in two steps. First, upon the advice of a clergy friend, I stepped out of the pulpit and told a story without notes during part of the sermon. I received such rave reviews from that experiment that I decided to try preaching the next Sunday without notes and doing so outside of the pulpit. Again, I received an enthusiastic endorsement of the new style from countless members of the congregation. After that Sunday, I never returned to a manuscript. In fact, in short order I skipped manuscripting all together, choosing only to do sequencing of the components of the sermon. Each person must decide if abandoning the manuscript is a good idea or not.

PERFECTING THE ART

If one is serious about learning to preach without notes, I heartily recommend Webb's book, *Preaching without Notes*. Several books are available, but I favor his to all I have read. If I can learn to preach without notes, surely most will be able to do so. I was so forgetful in junior high school that I had to write myself notes to remind myself to take my lunch money. No great memory here! I took up preaching without notes after thirty years of manuscript preaching. Once converting to this method I have been able to continue it even after fully entering the "forgetful" stage of adult life. The biggest hurdle is not in developing the memory skills, but in managing the fear and anxiety of not having a crutch to rely on. It is indeed "preaching without a net."

Those wishing to make the transition might try it as I did, in stages—first only doing part of the sermon without notes, next with a note card in hand and finally with no card at all. Webb's book makes this transition much easier by taking the new recruit through all the basics—even addressing the fear and anxiety of the new method.

ORAL WRITING

I would later add one more technique to preaching without notes—oral writing. By this I mean no manuscripting at all and very few sentences ever written down. I would decide on the sequences and then "write" the sermon in my head by simply talking through the sermon, not one time but five or six times. I would often change the sequence in the process and sometimes even the ending. By Friday I usually would make a final memory card and then work from that forward.

FINAL PREPARATIONS

Assuming that some of the readers are ready to preach "without a net," I will be sharing how I prepare for that scary task. In the last page of this book I have included my Memory Card for the last sermon of the book, "Hey! Where's my Gold Star?" Listed below are the major rules I follow:

MEMORY CARD

- Half of an 8 ½ x 11 page.
- Set margins (Top, .5; Bottom, 1; Left, 1.5; Right 2.6)
- Illustrations, numbers, symbols down the left margin. These remind me of those component parts. I use different colors to aid my recall.
- Main headings in all caps and bolded, placed just to the right of the illustrations
- Sub points or details under each component part
- No sentences, only phrases (There is not enough room and you will be looking down only for the idea or phrase, not the sentence.)
- Ending has exact wording of last two lines of the sermon.

The next issue is what to do with the memory card. Since it is a half sheet, it fits well into a Bible. Often I carry the Bible with me and have the memory card on top or inside the Bible. I can refer to it if I need to, but rarely do so. Since I often preach in the chancel area, I can place the memory card on the communion table or the end of the communion rail. If a book is quoted, I take the book with me and the note card is inside it or on top of it. When I do the quote, I take a quick glance down at the note card to refresh my memory.

When I first start practicing the sermon, I use the memory card as a prompt for my speaking. By Saturday I try practicing without using the memory card. I usually forget a part of the sermon at that stage, which is really a positive because I am not likely to forget that part on Sunday. By Sunday I have the sequence in my brain, in my speaking memory, and I have the picture of that memory card with all the colors and symbols emblazoned on my mind. I suppose one could say that I always preach with notes; it is just that the "notes" are in my head.

MANUSCRIPT OPTION

If you never venture out into the world of preaching without notes, you can still adopt some of its techniques. Your manuscript can have symbols and drawings in the margins just like the cards. When I did manuscript preaching, I used this method which allowed me to glance down at my colored drawings and look back up with the story in my mind. The goal was not to look down at the text but only at the illustration.

In my experience, if I produced a polished manuscript, I still had the "literary style" in my head. I talked more like I was reading than talking. I got complaints from some members who said I "read" my sermon. Of course, this was not true at all, but it was the way it sounded to them. A special nuance was added to my preaching when I made the second step to "oral composition." With that method of preparation I could not preach in a "literary style" since I had created and shaped the sermon only using an oral or conversational style.

REHEARSE THE SERMON

Whether you preach from a manuscript, from notes, or with no prompts at all, practicing without notes early in the process can be helpful. Whenever possible I try to practice the final few times in the setting where I will preach and with the microphone I will use. This becomes a part of the memory. I also practice with pauses. A wise use of silence can be most effective in preaching, allowing time for people to mull over an idea or to absorb emotional impact. Later, those pauses may even help when it takes a few seconds to recall the next segment of your sermon. Once I forgot my progression and just paused and stared at the audience. Within seconds—that seemed like minutes—I regained my "place" and continued on. One lady grabbed me after the service and said enthusiastically, "Boy, that dramatic pause was so effective!" I thanked her warmly for her comment.

LAST MINUTE ADJUSTMENTS

When one preaches without notes or with only a memory card, it is very easy to make changes and then write the revisions on the card. Many of my memory cards have an extra phrase at the bottom, a sign of a revised ending. Sometimes the idea would come to me between services, and I would just make a notation on the card. Sometimes those last-minute changes became the best part of the sermon. With "oral style" preaching, one can never be "finished" with the sermon on Thursday when the manuscript is written. It is only becomes the "sermon" when it is preached. Remember the sermon is a "spoken" and not a "written" word. It only becomes a sermon when it is "heard."

STAND AND DELIVER

Finally, that time arrives and we stand to preach. Surely a prayer is fitting whether spoken out loud or whispered from our seat before rising. The Spirit has work to do with us and certainly with each person who will hear. I am grateful that the Spirit is working on my behalf and God's behalf to ensure that some significant word is heard during those preaching moments. I offer my sermon with three persons as my audience. I offer the sermon to God, to the congregation, and to myself. When people tell me that I was speaking straight to them in the sermon I often reply, "Well, I was really preaching to myself, but it's good that some of you get caught in the crossfire!"

PREACHING OUTSIDE THE PULPIT?

I have found that stepping outside of the pulpit helps me be more present to the congregation. Something happens when I leave the comfort zone of the pulpit. My sense of vulnerability helps foster the preacher/listener connection. If, however, the stepping into the chancel becomes the preacher's opportunity to "showboat" or "entertain," then I strongly recommend a quick return to the pulpit. If the space or sound system requires that I stay in the pulpit, then I try not to resort to old habits and look down at my notes. I always remain in the pulpit for funerals and other services where my presence out front would be a distraction. Each preacher will have to decide what style works best.

NOTES

1. Joseph M. Webb, *Preaching without Notes* (Nashville: Abingdon Press, 2001), p. 20.
2. Ibid. p. 21.
3. William J. Carl, III, ed., *Best Advice* (Louisville, Kentucky: Westminster John Knox Press, 2009), pp. 94-95.

CHAPTER EIGHT

ATTENTION TO DETAIL

BEGINNINGS

Most preachers know that the beginning of the sermon is extremely important. Unfortunately, many believe that the most important effect is simply to "catch the attention" of the audience. Of course, a well-timed explosion, shrill whistle, or intense flash of light can bring people to spell-bounding attention—but that will not invite the listener into the space of the sermon. Instead of trying to "get people's attention" the preacher should deftly point the listener toward the goal of the sermon. This can be accomplished with a whisper or a shout, with bells and whistles or the hush of angel wings. No sonic boom is required.

ESSENTIAL INGREDIENTS

Engage the Listener

Whatever else a beginning accomplishes, it must *engage* the listener. The hearer might be invited to take a journey, explore the hidden depths of the faith, or wrestle with life's tough exegetical questions. The purpose of the beginning is to invite the listener to become an *insider* rather than a spectator, to be a part of the conversation rather than a passive recipient of some "important information." When the beginning works well, the preacher will be connected to the listener and the listener will be drawn into the sermon's focus.

Connect the Beginning to the Rest of the Sermon

The beginning is not a "warm up act" to be followed by the main attraction. It is more akin to the overture that precedes a musical—introducing the themes, suggesting the mood, and whetting the appetite for all that lies ahead. Season ticket holders know that whatever is introduced by the orchestra will be repeated and expanded in the unfolding drama. Good sermon beginnings do the same: they set the mood, introduce the theme and invite the hearer into the midst of the story.

PRACTICES TO AVOID

Preachers are notorious for passing down bad habits to future generations and although the new subscribers instinctively know these techniques are not working, many refuse to look for fresh alternatives.

Statement of Topic

I hope in a day of visual overload and short attention spans that few preachers will succumb to the old practice of beginning the sermon by simply announcing the topic. "Today I want to talk to you about love." I can hear the listener's brain shifting gears to the passive mode, trying to prepare for what will surely be a series of points that the preacher will ration out to the needy parishioners. Meanwhile the hearer's subconscious is whispering a warning: "This will just be a sermon 'about' love. Don't get too excited. Just try to pay attention. Don't worry; I see no hint that it will get personal."

Holbert's "No Fly" List

John Holbert in the book *What Not to Say* shares several types of beginnings that should be quickly discarded. Like a "statement of topic" beginning, they have been used by hundreds of preachers, but popular usage is no guarantee of effectiveness. Here is a listing of Holbert's banned practices for beginnings: [1] (The commentary under each bullet is mine.)

- **Do not "Overcute" Yourself at the Start**
  Some preachers try to use a cute story to "warm up" the listener. Unfortunately, this "light" beginning will not likely match the tone of the remainder of the sermon, creating a disconnect. Even worse, a cute story may tend to trivialize what will follow.

- **Do not Tell a Joke to Start Your Sermon**
  Yes, I have told a joke at the first of the sermon—but not often. It is not enough that the joke contains a word or phrase that will be used in the body of the sermon. It needs to lead naturally into the body of the sermon and set the tone for the day.

- **Do not Tell a Long Emotional Story at the Start**
  As a rule the preacher should not invite the hearer into a deep emotional mood at the start. Such stories are suited better toward the end. One may, however, raise deep and troubling issues at the start—the goal being to raise the issue without pulling the listener into an emotional tailspin.

- **Do Not *Blither* Into the Sermon**
  Like Holbert, I love the sound of the word "blither." It reminds me a bit of *blabber* and *blunder*—both capturing the essence of an inept beginning. How tragic when a preacher stumbles onto the stage with no opening lines prepared, being content to simply *blither* on about his trip to the church that morning or yesterday's ballgame. Rather than connecting with the listener with such "small talk," the preacher has lowered the expectations of the listener who had actually hoped for an inspiring message. The hearer can only hope the preacher will find a quick transition into the text or the main message.

TULL'S BEGINNINGS

In an effort to share a variety of beginnings, I have noted below beginning excerpts from two of my books of sermons. Some proceed directly from the text while others begin with an exegetical question. Hopefully, all have the power to engage the ones gathered to hear.

From *Wrestlings, Wonders, and Wanderers* [2]

The Agonizing Provider (Genesis 22:1-128)

Today we look again at Abraham. We remember God's promise of a great nation, a new land and numerous descendents. We remember God's plan to bless all of humanity through him and his people. So we have a right to be thoroughly confused and confounded with the passage before us. Here in Genesis 22, God asks Abraham to offer his only son as a burnt offering.

Stairways of Heaven (Genesis 28:10-17)

As I studied in depth the passage of scripture, I learned that I have long carried misconceptions about "Jacob's ladder." My first surprising discovery was that all the commentaries I read suggested that Jacob's vision was not of a ladder as we know it today, but more of a "ramp" or "stair-like pavement." This ramp was to handle traffic between heaven and earth. Heavenly messengers could approach thereby those dwelling below.

Hip Pointer! (Genesis 22:1-128)

Our narrative begins with Jacob's sending his family across the Jabbok stream while staying behind to spend the night alone. Tomorrow he must face his brother, Esau, whom he has not seen since he escaped after stealing Esau's blessing and having fleeced him out of his birthright. Jacob does not know how his brother will receive him...but several possibilities have occurred to him—none of them good. It should come as no surprise that Jacob got little sleep that night. Who could sleep well, knowing that one must stand in front of an angry brother and beg for forgiveness?

From *Why God Why?* [3]

Why, God, Why? (Philippians 4:4-6)

Have you ever asked the question, "Why, God, why?" Have you ever asked, "Why did this have to happen to me?" or "Why did God allow this to happen to my friend?" Have you ever wondered if people really deserve all the bad things that come their way? If you have asked one or all of these questions, you join millions who when faced with tragic circumstances raise their cries of agony, or confusion, or protest to God.

Everything Working for Good? (Romans 8:28)

In Romans 8:28 Paul makes perhaps the most daring claim of his ministry! It is a claim he makes not only for himself, but also on behalf of the Christians in Rome. Some would argue he even speaks for us when he says, "We know that all things work together for good for those who love God, who are called according to his purpose." Can we really believe that no matter how bad things seem right now, God will work with us to ensure that things work out for good? Is this just wishful thinking or is it gospel?

Earthen Vessels (2 Corinthians 4:7-9)

This sermon is a narrative. The text will be illustrated through the wrestlings of a young woman that I will call Susan. Some might argue that Susan never existed, that her story is neither believable nor true. But I have known many a Susan. In fact, I have even felt like Susan at various times in my life. You may be certain. Susan is real.

Blessed Thorn! (2 Corinthians 12:7-10)

In his letter to the church at Corinth, Paul comes dangerously close to giving thanks for something he called a "thorn in the flesh." Though he did not welcome the thorn, Paul admitted that he had benefitted from it. He said that it kept him from being "too elated." It helped him to be more humble. What was this thorn in the flesh? Why did Paul ask for it to be removed? Why did Paul eventually become accepting of it, and even see it as a "blessing in disguise"?

Living with Critics! (1 Corinthians. 4:3-4)

Have you ever received any criticism? Has negative criticism ever gotten under your skin? Have you spent too much of your life trying to please your critics? What would you really like to say to your greatest critic—maybe an overly critical parent, an aggressive spouse, a persistent boss, or a belligerent enemy?

Beyond Positive Thinking! (Philippians 4-8)

Would our lives be any different if we decided to take the National Enquirer's view of life instead of heeding Paul's advice? Paul tells us that we are to contemplate the "true, honorable, just, pure, lovely, and gracious." Would we be any different if we chose instead to think on the scandalous, the racy, the perverted, the bizarre, the ugly, the caustic, and the sensational? Both of these options have their appeal. One offers excitement and piques our curiosity—"inquiring minds want to know." The other speaks a message of hope and wholeness and peace.

Beginnings are extremely important. What happens in the first two minutes of the sermon may well determine how many listeners will stay for the whole message and how many will begin composing a mental "to do list" or deciding what restaurant to go to following the service. So, preachers beware! Choose those first phrases very carefully!

ATTENTION TO DETAIL

ENDINGS

The ending of the sermon is even more crucial than its beginning. The ending is where the preacher stops the car and says goodbye to the listener. The journey is now over. The ending often determines if the destination is reached or if one remains stranded not really knowing how to make it back home.

It is always preferable to get off to a good start, but even more advantageous to finish well, to offer the worshipper a carryout bag to take home, providing future nourishment for the coming week. The ending needs to be strong, but what are the keys to its doing the job well? Here are a few key ingredients to a successful finish.

ESSENTIAL INGREDIENTS

It Completes the Narrative

The ending needs to finish the narrative. It should complete what was started with the beginning of the sermon and offer a type of closure. On rare occasions the sermon may seem to end with the sermon hanging in mid air. Hopefully, these abrupt endings will actually involve the preacher allowing the listeners to complete the message for themselves.

It Reflects the Sermon's Purpose

What is the sermon's intent? If it is to ask the listener for a decision, then the ending must accomplish that purpose. If the intent is to make an affirmation, then the ending should do just that. The last few lines of the sermon should carry with them the main thrust of the sermon!

The Listener is invited to embody the message

The last act of the preacher may well be to place the sermon in the hands of the hearer with the hopes it will be carried out the door and into daily life. Sermons that offer no challenge, that invite no decision, have squandered a great opportunity. Sermons should not be preached with the intention of "informational transmission" but rather for "transformational intention."

CRADDOCK'S LIST OF THIRTEEN ENDINGS

Fred Craddock offers a wide variety of formulas for ending the sermon. I share only descriptions of the various endings here, but the entire discussion can be found in *Craddock on the Craft of Preaching.* [4]

- End the sermon as it began
- End with a simple exhortation
- End with repetition and summary
- End with a choral response
- End with an appropriate prayer
- End with an invitation
- End with a story
- End a sermon with silence
- End with a question
- End with a fractured syllogism
- End with a refrain
- End with a broken sentence
- Deliver the one-half of the sermon and then let the people create the second half.

ENDINGS TO AVOID

Alas, awkward and ill-planned endings have seriously weakened what otherwise would have been a good sermon with positive impact. Several bad habits have left many listeners ready to sign up their pastor for a week-long preaching seminar. Here are only a few of the worst offenders:

False Endings ("Cruel Tease Endings")

Not long ago Alyce McKenzie provided me with one of my favorite analogies for those who cannot finish a sermon or end a protracted story. If feedback is allowed, one only has to make an impassioned plea: "Land the plane. Land the plane!" McKenzie insists that too many preachers pass up perfect landings for their sermons only to lift off the runway and circle around for another pass. Hearers know instinctively when the message has been concluded. When a powerful story is told near the end of the allotted time, the audience begins to fold their bulletins and reach for their coats. But the preacher is unaware that half of the congregation has made a mental exit and continues on, trying to explain the story or even worse introducing another theme. Then finally—and we do hope *finally*—the preacher offers yet another dramatic ending, but this time the audience is not so receptive. For them the sermon ended two minutes ago, and the force of the first story and its poignancy has now been replaced with irritation. "Land the plane, preacher. Land the plane. [5]

It is almost always preferable to choose between two endings than to try stacking them on top of each other at the close. Avoid false ending at all costs. Thomas Long speaks the truth when he writes, "Sermon conclusions that come after the hearers have finished listening can only serve as pallbearers." [6]

Backing over the Spikes

Alyce McKenzie also warns against endings that "back over the spikes." [7] Some preachers, as they near the end of their sermon, decide that the listener needs a complete review of the sermon, so they put the sermon in reverse backing over grace and arriving back at sin and confession. Rather than preparing the listener to go forth in grace, they remind the parishioner again of their shortcomings. Sermon endings need to move forward, not backward. They need to move from reflection to action instead of retracing their steps. It is better to "spare" oneself a possible blowout. Keep the sermon in *drive* until the very end!

High Sugar, Low Nutrition Endings

I still remember the ploy of newscasts using puppies or pandas to add "sweetness" to a newscast otherwise filled with crimes and disasters. It never worked for me. Preachers can succumb to the same temptation and try to share "feel good stories" to brighten up their sermons. Many save the "high fructose" variety for the ending, leaving the listeners not with a model for living but with a sugar high that will dissipate before they can shake the preacher's hand following the service. Better we follow the new model in newscasts today, closing with real stories of real people making a real difference. Now, that makes me feel better—and also ready to do the same.

TULL'S ENDINGS

Listed below are a variety of endings, taken from the same sermon books utilized in the previous section on beginnings. They offer a variety of styles and invite different responses from the listener.

From *Wrestlings, Wonders, and Wanderers* [8]

The Agonizing Provider (Genesis 22:1-128)

God always has been the Great Provider. God provides for us in the midst of our abundance. God provides for us in the midst of our agony, our time of temptation, our hour of despair. God celebrates with us when our joys triumph over our fears. So when trials come, when agony appears, when temptation knocks, remember the words of Abraham: "God will provide." God will provide indeed!

The Birthright Blues! (Genesis 25:19-34)

So what will it be for you? Will you cast your pearls before swine, sell your birthright for a cup of chili, bury your talent or use it, be grateful for all that has been given you or pout in the corner until you win the lottery? Will you live only for the moment, care more about food and money than meaning and purpose, value life or devalue it? Let me make it simple for you now: What will your autobiography be titled: *Birthright Blues* or *Birthday Bonanza?*

Stairways of Heaven (Genesis 28:10-17)

So the next time we are on the run, the next time fear has the best of us, the next time we feel lost in a foreign land, let us remember Jacob's dream and the promise of God's presence. We should not be surprised to find God there. Heaven and earth meet not once but many times. So on our journey, as we fall into the pit or as we climb higher and higher to get a glimpse of God, we should not be surprised to discover that "Behold, the God of Jacob...is already with us!"

Hip Pointer (Genesis 22:1-128)

As we struggle with life, we need not quit. We have the presence and power of God to see us through. So hang in, hold on, and hang tough. A blessing is on its way!

From *Why God Why?* [9]

Why, God, Why? (Philippians 4:4-6)

Perhaps you and I do not ask "Why God why?" too often. Perhaps we ask the question too seldom. Maybe we can agree to a rule for its usage: "when sorrow comes, we have no right to ask, 'Why did this happen to me?' unless we ask the same question whenever joy comes our way."

Earthen Vessels (2 Corinthians 4:7-9))

At sixteen Jason was just beginning to understand what had eluded Susan for almost forty-four years. He now knew that we are all vulnerable. We can be battered, hurt, betrayed. Life teaches us: earthen vessels are destined to break. But Jason had also come to believe that when they break, there is a power, a transcendent power, offered to us!

Jason arranged the potted flowers on his mother's grave. It was their secret symbol—two cracked clay pots at the foot of her grave, two pots with yellow mums bursting into full bloom.

Jason now shared Susan's priceless discovery. But Susan's witness of faith had first been Paul's witness to the church at Corinth: "We have this treasure in earthen vessels to show that the transcendent power belongs to God and not to us" (2 Corinthians 4:7 RSV).

Blessed Thorn! (2 Corinthians 12:7-10)

That really is the bottom line. Is God's grace sufficient for you or not? Is God's grace sufficient even with the nagging thorns in your side, the aggravating splinters in your hands? Just tell me, "Is God's grace sufficient?"

ILLUSTRATIONS

A PARADIGM SHIFT

Thomas Long in his book, *The Witness of Preaching*, discusses the evolution of the use of illustrations within the sermon. Decades ago an illustration was often used to "shed light" on the logical argument of the preacher.[10] It was a way to "flesh out" ideas that were a bit abstract and without total clarity. With the demise of deductive preaching with its points and logical arguments came new possibilities of how the preacher might use illustrative material. Craddock rightly suggests that a good preacher no longer has to sprinkle illustrations throughout the sermon to make it either interesting or clear. Craddock makes his argument:

> In the proper sense of the term, an illustration refers to that which illumines or clarifies what has been said another way. Recall, for example, the pictures along with the text in public school books. The presence of an illustration assumes that for some, at least, the text alone may not be clear. However, a sermon may not need illustrations. If it possessed unity of thought, movement toward its goal, and language lively and imaginative, parishioners may speak of the sermon's illustrations when, in fact, there were none. The whole sermon was illumined and clear. Just as some very humorous people seldom if ever tell jokes, just as good storytellers do not have to tell stories all the time, so the preacher who leads the listeners down interesting and well-lighted streets does not have to load the sermon with illustrations.
>
> Actually, in good preaching what is referred to as illustrations are, in fact, stories or anecdotes which do not illustrate the point rather they *are* the point.[11]

MY BIAS AGAINST "CANNED" ILLUSTRATIONS

I share with Craddock a basic distrust for books entitled "*101 Great Sermon Illustrations.*" Most of these books, which contain what I call "canned" illustrations, do not yield a full 101 usable illustrations but more likely only three or four. The rest are too trite, too inept, or lack theological soundness. They are often heavy on emotion, and light on substance. Their "happy endings" rely more on a change of circumstances than a transformation of the person. I have a much better success in using literature where the illustrative material is not "set aside" but is instead nestled inside of biographies, novels or magazine articles. In them I am most likely to find a "slice of life" which I can carefully insert into the sermon's narrative.

Using "canned illustrations" is akin to buying mediocre potato salad at the grocery delicatessen to add to a home-made main dish. It looks all right on the menu, but it does not measure up to the meal it is supposed to enhance. Unless I can find an unusually good illustration, one resembling the gourmet offerings at top-end super markets, I will have to look elsewhere for a life scenario worthy of my worshipping guests.

LITMUS TESTS FOR ILLUSTRATIVE MATERIAL

Perhaps sermon illustrations should have to past a litmus test for their appropriateness before they can be added to the sermon's menu. Here are my top three tests:

If it doesn't fit, you've got to omit!

I don't care how great an illustration it is. If it does not fit the sermon, then save it, put it on the shelf until it fits perfectly another sermon. Too many preachers try to use a newly discovered illustration as soon as possible as if it had a short expiration date. Better to wait.

If it is not true to life, it won't seem true to the listener!

I have heard miraculous illustrations about people praying for a specific need and on the last day of a deadline a check comes in the mail for the exact amount. It does not matter whether or not the story actually happened—it certainly might be a true account. Even so, for the story to ring true to me or to the listener, the account needs to be believable, to be consistent with the hearer's own experience.

Does the illustration reflect sound theology?

Another important test for all illustrations is to ask what theology is being offered. Stories of miraculous healings have certainly been documented, but what is the purpose of using them as illustrations? What theology of prayer or healing is being suggested? In the congregation will be people who have lost spouses to cancer. No amount of praying brought physical healing to their loved one. A better illustration, one with a more sound theology, would be a story of spiritual healing— someone who faced cancer and death and was defeated by neither. Illustrations should not be picked on the basis of emotional impact but rather upon the message they are sending to the person in the pew.

BEST SOURCE FOR ILLUSTRATIVE MATERIAL: LIFE

I have found the best source for illustrative material is not from books but from the experiences of life itself. We preachers would be wrong to go through life *shopping* for illustrations. To do so would lessen their value, like taking a picture of a sunset to show to others but never being awed by the view. Even so, the preacher will experience ample poignant moments in the midst of ministry that may be seen as "signs of the kingdom" or "means of grace." My favorite preachers are those who have more stories, more life scenarios than they can use even if they were to preach every day. They have an eye for grace and ears always open to that kernel of truth. They are students of the Bible, to be sure. But they are also students of life, and very few hallowed moments pass before them without their notice.

Fred Craddock is one such masterful collector of life—life that reflects the Gospel. In a collection of his stories I have many favorites. One has no title, but I call it "Joy Tired." I include it below and with it Craddock's reflection of the event. It sounds to me like a perfect ending to a sermon.

> I recall some years ago in a church I was visiting on a Sunday afternoon, a van pulled up in the church parking lot, and a bunch of young people got out. They looked like thirteen, fourteen, fifteen, maybe up to eighteen years old. I think there were ten or twelve young people who belonged to that church. They got out with bedrolls. It was the awfullest looking bunch of kids you've ever seen, something like the cats would drag in. They were really in bad shape. I said, "What it this?" They had just returned from a work mission. They named the place where they went. In one week, those young people, along with other young people, had built a little church for the community. They were beat. Aw, they looked terrible.
>
> They were sitting on their bags out there waiting for their parents to come. I said to one of the boys, I said, "You tired?" and he said, "Whew—am I tired!" Then he said, "This is the best tired I've ever felt."
>
> Now that's what joy is. Do you feel that? "This is the best tired I've ever felt." I hope some day young people in this church get that tired. I hope we all get that tired. The best tired there is, is called in your Bible, joy. [12]

CREATE YOUR OWN ILLUSTRATION

In my last sermon in the book, "Hey! Where's my Gold Star?," I use a story of my own creation to complete the narrative and bring home the main point of the sermon. Craddock, in a similar way, often uses his imagination to craft the perfect story for his sermon narrative. One of my favorite examples of such imagination is the one I have listed below. His playful imagination makes the listener smile while providing a full dose of insight. I once used this illustration in a sermon entitled "Rat Race Retirement." As you will notice, the illustration even inspired my choice of title.

You can't teach an old dog new tricks. Wrong. If you believe in God, you can teach an old dog new tricks. I've never been to the greyhound races, but I've seen them on TV. They have these beautiful old dogs—I say beautiful, they are really ugly—big dogs, and they run that mechanical rabbit around the ring, and these dogs just run, exhausting themselves chasing it. When those dogs get to where they can't race, the owners put a little ad in the paper, and if anybody wants one for a pet, they can have it; otherwise they are going to be destroyed. I have a niece in Arizona who can't stand that ad. She goes and gets them. Big old dogs in the house; she loves them.

I was in the home not long ago where they'd adopted a dog that had been a racer. It was a big old greyhound, spotted hound, lying there in the den. One of the kids in the family, just a toddler, was pulling on its tail and a little older kid had his head on that old dog's stomach, used it for a pillow. That dog just seemed so happy, and I said to the dog,

"Uh, are you still racing any?"

"No, I don't race anymore."

"Do you miss the glitter and excitement of the track?"

"No, no, I still had run in me."

"Well did you not win?"

He said, *"I won over a million dollars for my owner."*

"Then what was it, bad treatment?"

"Oh no, they treated us royally when we were racing."

I said, ""Then what? Did you get crippled?"

He said, *"No, no, no."*

I said, "Then what?"

And he said, *"I quit."*

"You quit?"

"Yeah, that's what I said. I quit."

I Said, "Why did you quit?"

And he said, *"I discovered that what I was chasing was not really a rabbit. And I quit."* He looked at me and said, *"All that running, running, running, running, and what I was chasing was not even real."* [13]

SERMON TITLES

KEY FUNCTION

I once heard of a minister who spent hours each week deciding on the exact title for the sermon. I would think that such a huge block of time would be better spent selecting an appropriate "form" for the sermon or in crafting a powerful ending. Even so, I am not ready to dismiss the sermon title as having limited value. It can still pique the interest, point to a central theme or give a framework for the sermon and thus provide the listener with a handy "memory device." I can still remember sermon titles of ten, twenty, and even forty years ago and with them the main gist of the sermon.

If one cannot be creative or at least a bit dramatic, I would prefer no title at all. The title should not just list a topic but give a hint of the particular focus. Sometimes, a title just provokes curiosity. One warning: make sure the title is connected to the sermon itself. False advertizing creates bad PR with the congregation. Here are some of my own creations:

TULL'S TITLES

- *Frogs, Warm Fuzzies and Cold Pricklies?*
- *Tit for Tat, not That!*
- *Salvation: Freeze-Dried or Fresh Perked?*
- *Hell, Fire, and Tombstones!*
- *A Plea for Nine Commandments!*
- *Hey! Where's My Gold Star?* (Luke 17;1-10)
- *Rat Race Retirement!* (Isaiah 55:1-3a; 1 Cor. 9:24-27)
- *Eat, Drink, and Remember!* (a title for a communion sermon)
- *Playing Church or Seeking God?*
- *Born from Above Christians!* (John 3:1-6)
- *Is Christianity the Only Way?*

ATTENTION TO DETAIL

- *Lighter with More Weight!* (Matthew 11:28-30)
- *What will it be, Mary or Martha?* (Luke 10:38-42)
- *The Birthright Blues!* (Genesis 25:19-34)
- *God of all the Nations* (Acts 10:34-43)
- *Prayer: Beyond a Genie Mentality!*
- *How to Treat Your Minister!*

Sermon titles are just one more way a preacher can use imagination. It can be a helpful exercise of wit and intellect that hopefully will be replicated in the sermon itself.

NOTES

1. John C. Holbert and Alyce M. McKenzie, *What Not to Say* (Louisville Kentucky: Westminster John Knox Press, 2011), pp. 37-39.
2. Justin W. Tull, *Wrestlings, Wonders, and Wanderers* (Lima, Ohio: C.S.S. Publishing Company, 1992), pp. 27, 41, 47.
3. Justin W. Tull, *Why God, Why? Sermons on the Problem of Pain* (Nashville: Abingdon Press, 1996) pp. 9, 24, 38, 46, 53, 69.
4. Lee and Kathryn Hayes Sparkes, ed., *Craddock on the Craft of Preaching* (St. Louis, Missouri: Chalice Press: 2011), p. 54.
5. McKenzie, *What Not to Say*, p. 105.
6. Thomas G. Long, *The Witness of Preaching* (Louisville: Westminster John Knox Press, 2005), p. 192.
7. McKenzie, *What Not to Say*, p. 107.
8. Tull, *Wrestlings, Wonders, and Wanderers*, pp. 33, 39, 46, 53, 60.
9. Tull, *Why God, Why?*, pp. 16, 45, 52.
10. Long, p. 201.
11. Fred Craddock, *Preaching* (Nashville: Abingdon Press, 1985), p. 204
12. Mike Graves and Richard F. Ward, ed., *Craddock Stories* (St. Louis Missouri: Chalice Press, 2001), p. 94.
13. Ibid. pp 106-107.

CHAPTER NINE

SERMONS AND COMMENTARY

Homiletical theory, which we have explored extensively in this book, can challenge the preacher to think in new ways, but these new insights can easily remain just that—theory—until they are "fleshed out" in actual sermons, first, perhaps, with others leading the way, and then put into practice by ourselves. In this section I will share a collection of sermons containing a diversity of style, form, sermon content, and intended purpose. Following each sermon I will give a brief commentary referencing the purpose, context and techniques involved. In some cases the congregation had no critical need that required being addressed. At other times, however, the sermon was intentionally crafted with a particular congregational need in mind. Preaching should endeavor to address both—the critical issues of Church life, and matters that are centered in daily Christian living. Paul, in his work with the early church, seemed to follow a similar pattern. Sometimes, it is obvious that he is addressing a critical church problem. At other times, his message seems more general as when laying out a particular theological concept or in addressing issues of Christian behavior. Two of the sermons included here were specifically designed for churches in the midst of severe crisis. The others could be preached in a variety of settings and circumstances.

I hope by offering these sermons of diverse style and form that preachers will be encouraged to develop new techniques and sharpen older ones, and in the process reaffirm their commitment to pursuing excellence in the awesome task of sharing God's word.

Christmas at Ramah!

Matthew. 2:16-18

When Herod saw that he had been tricked by the wise men, he was infuriated, and he sent and killed all the children in and around Bethlehem who were two years old or under, according to the time that he had learned from the wise me. Then was fulfilled what had been spoken through the prophet Jeremiah:
"A voice was heard in Ramah,
Wailing and loud lamentation,
Rachel weeping for her children,
She refused to be consoled,
Because they are no more."

Have you ever spent Christmas at Ramah? Have you ever heard mothers crying over the loss of their children? Have you ever had trouble receiving the good news of Jesus' birth because you were lonely, depressed, or grieving?

Christmas comes every year to Ramah. It comes to all cities and villages. It comes to anyone who will welcome the news of the Christ Child, and to those who receive its message there comes a deep joy, a joy even through tears!

In the Gospel of Matthew we are told the story of King Herod commanding the killing in Bethlehem of all male children two years and younger. Matthew follows the story with these words from Jeremiah:

"A voice was heard in Ramah, wailing and loud lamentation,
Rachel weeping for her children; she refused to be consoled,
because they were no more." (Matt. 2:18)

Rachel, as you may recall, was the mother of Joseph and Benjamin and thus the ancestress of the children of Israel. In the book of Jeremiah, Rachel was weeping for her children in exile. But here her spirit weeps for the babies killed by Herod's men and for the families who lost them. Ramah is not far from Bethlehem where the soldiers performed their terrible deed. Surely weeping and wailing could be heard throughout the countryside.

As I reflected upon this text, I detected a double tragedy. First was the tragedy of the slaughter of infants, infants who meant no harm, infants innocent of adult scheming and wickedness. What indeed could be more tragic than the loss of these little ones?

This initial tragedy, however, does not compare to the tragedy that follows, which is that the grief never ends. These mothers are never consoled. There will be no light to cast out the darkness. Despair will defeat hope! What word can we bring to these grieving mothers of Bethlehem? It was Jesus' birth that led to the death of their sons. Will the Christmas story remain a nightmare to them? Will it offer no hope? Will they never understand that Jesus came bringing life, not death; that he gives hope, not despair, that he wipes away tears and shares with us a deep and abiding joy?

Can the angels' song be heard from Bethlehem to Ramah? Will the echo of "Gloria" hush their crying? Must one tragedy be followed by another? Will those who grieve refuse to be consoled? It is tragic to lose a child, but must they lose the Christ Child also? It is tragic to lose a spouse, but must one also forfeit the joy of Christmas? It is tragic to observe human suffering, but must that suffering rob us of hope?

The Christ Child comes to Ramah and to Bethlehem. This holy child will suffer no harm for now, but he will later know much suffering. He will later experience human sorrow. But this child was born to bring joyous life: abundant life and life eternal. No tragedy can destroy that good news!

Yet today Ramah is with us. Innocent children still die in Bethlehem, and in India, and across our land. Good people still get sick. Saints of the church still die. There is still crying around us as we again prepare to sing "Joy to the World."

As Christians we may not always have a "Holly, Jolly Christmas," for much may sadden us. We can still have a joyous Christmas, a hopeful Christmas, one that is not afraid to embrace sadness with loving compassion, to smile in the midst of our tears, to worship a Savior who can defeat our tragedy.

Christians can speak of joy when all is not joyful. They can announce the "light of the world" when there is still much darkness. They can offer love and hope to the mothers and fathers of Bethlehem and Ramah and even of our city. Yes, tragedy is forever with us. The innocent suffer. But as Christians we are ready and willing to be consoled. We do not desire to stay in our tombs or to feed on the darkness. In the midst of our darkness we may see clearly the Natal Star!

This year Christmas comes to many with heavy hearts. Some have lost loved ones. Some fear they may soon lose the ones they love. Some have concerns and anxieties over loved ones. Some are ill; and some are lonely.

If we have heavy hearts, *Jingle Bells* will probably not console us. But can we remain hopeless amid candlelight and the words and melody of *Silent Night?* Can we remain joyless as the faithful of our church sing *Joy to the World?* An Advent devotion by Margret Huffman offers us some hope for a joyful Christmas:

> Is this the year when the joys of Christmas sound only as empty echoes in a once-happy marriage, split by divorce or death? Sadnesses are magnified at this time of year, when everything seems larger than life—even emptiness.

> It was such a year for the young woman who had suffered just about all there was to endure: illness, the death of her remaining parent, the end of a relationship. There was no way she could even imagine celebrating Christmas—until early in December, she received a brightly wrapped package from a friend. Inside was a tiny gold Christmas-tree lapel

pin, with a note: "Wishing you even a little Christmas." "And that was all the Christmas I could celebrate that year," she explained, pointing to the minute gold pin on her lapel, where it has rested each holiday since that darkest one.

"Some years, once again, it is about all I can muster, but a 'little Christmas' is always enough," she added. Yet isn't just a fragment of hope better that none? Isn't a tiny celebration better than a dark, empty room? For isn't it sufficient to have faith as a mustard seed? For from such small seeds of faith can grow Christmas truths of all sizes, nourished sometimes by our own tears of pain.

No matter what pain might be preventing you from celebrating this year, imagine a tiny gold Christmas tree, pinned right there on your lapel. Then look in the mirror and wish yourself, "Merry Christmas, anyway." [1]

This year the Christ Child promises to come to Ramah and Bethlehem. The Christ Child will come where angels sing and mothers cry. This Christ promises us joy, a joy not filled with frivolous laughter but with a gladness that comes in the midst of our tears.

Tragedy will not come to everyone's door this year. Some of us have received good news. Some are recovering from illness. Some have had a close call with death and are now doing much better. Some of us have witnessed positive transformations in people we love and have a new hope for their future.

But all of us know those who live in Ramah this year. We all know of those who are hurting, so we may have compassion for them and reach out to them. But we need not be in total despair for them, for even in their situation there is hope. Perhaps we simply wish for them the brightest Christmas they can have. We say to them in our hearts, "Have a Merry Christmas, anyway!" And we are somehow consoled—as hopefully they are consoled—by the news of a Christ Child coming into our world and into our lives.

If you have ever experienced in your family the birth of a child or grandchild following the death of a family member, you know that such a new life brings a very special kind of joy. It is a joy that does not stop the tears, but it does wipe them away.

The gift of the Christ Child is such a gift. The Christ Child does not eliminate all tragedy, but he makes all tragedy infinitely more bearable, and he adds to our experience the welling up of a very deep joy.

Melvin Wheatley, in his marvelous book *Christmas Is for Celebrating*, teaches us that there is much to celebrate each and every Christmas:

> Not a world that has in it nothing but good, but a world that is
> good, while having in it so much that is bad;
> Not a life that know no darkness, but a life in which
> even those who walk in darkness have seen a great light;
> Not a God who gives us everything we want,
> but a God who gives us everything we have,
> and offers us all we need, now and forever. [2]

This year there will be crying in Ramah, Iran, Turkey, Afghanistan and the United States, and some of those crying will refuse to be consoled. Some will choose to double their tragedy because this Christmas they will not listen for the angels' song. They will not look for the light that shines in the darkness!

But to all who turn an ear toward Bethlehem's song, to all who follow a star in the midst of shadows, to all who listen for the word of good news, there will be a comfort and even more—there will be a deep, deep joy!

The wise men knew, the shepherds knew, the angels knew what we now know—that there is nothing that can happen that prevents God from consoling us. Whether you live in Ramah or Bethlehem or in this city, crying can be heard.

This Christmas the Christ Child comes to all of us—and when he comes he will never, never leave us.

Paul's Christmas card to us is quite unique. On the outside we see the image of Christ. On the inside we read these words:

> What then are we to say about these things? If God is for us, who is against us? . . . Who will separate us from the love of Christ? Will hardship, or distress, or persecution, or famine, or peril or sword?. . . No, in all these things we are more than conquerors through him who loved us. For I am convinced that neither death, nor life, nor angels, nor rulers, nor things present, nor things to come, nor powers, nor height, nor depth, nor anything else in all creation, will be able to separate us from the love of God in Christ Jesus our Lord. (Romans 8:31, 35, 37-39)

There is still crying in Bethlehem and Ramah. Good people still become ill. The saints still die. But the Christ Child still comes. The light still shines. And the darkness will never, never, never overcome it!

Excerpt from
Why God, Why? Sermons on the Problem of Pain by Dr. Justin Tull.

NOTES

1. Margaret Anne Huffman, *Advent, a Calendar of Devotions* (Nashville: The Upper Room, 1977), pp. 20-21.
2. Melvin Wheatley, *Christmas Is for Celebrating* (Nashville: The Upper Room, 1977), p. 22.

SERMON OVERVIEW

Sermon Sentence: *Christmas hope is always possible because the darkness cannot overcome Christ's light.*

Context: Eight church members had died in December.

Category of Sermon: Existential

Sermon Form: *Existential Question*

 First Christmas tragedy/ Wrestling with the present/ Final affirmation of hope

Techniques Used: Story/acknowledgement of a problem/ prose/ repeating of a theme/suggesting reasons for hope/final affirmation of hope

Purpose: To offer hope to those grieving, using the Advent Scripture and human example.

Ending: Strong affirmation that God's light can never be extinguished!

GENERAL COMMENTS

I preached this sermon first to a congregation who lost eight members in December. I could not preach "Have a Holly, Jolly Christmas." I had to address the experience of grief as we tried to celebrate the joy of Jesus' birth. The text with its tragic slaughtering of children gave me a poignant example of human suffering. The supplemental text from Isaiah provided a symbol of hope.

Many years later I would use only the last paragraph of this sermon as the close of my first sermon to a grieving church. Both church communities had suffered enormous grief. Both needed a word of hope in the midst of grief, a hope made real through the Christmas story. The words had a timeless message:

> There is still crying in Bethlehem. Good people become ill.
> The saints still die. But the Christ child still comes. The light

still shines. And the darkness will never, never, never overcome it.

Wise Men: Outsiders on the Inside

Matthew 2: 1–12

In the time of King Herod, after Jesus was born in Bethlehem of Judea, wise men from the East came to Jerusalem, asking, "Where is the child who has been born king of the Jews? For we observed his star at its rising, and have come to pay him homage." When King Herod heard this, he was frightened, and all Jerusalem with him; and calling together all the chief priests and scribes of the people, he inquired of them where the Messiah was to be born. They told him, "In Bethlehem of Judea; for so it has been written by the prophet: 'And you, Bethlehem, in the land of Judah, are by no means least among the rulers of Judah; for from you shall come a ruler who is to shepherd my people Israel.'" Then Herod secretly called for the wise men and learned from them the exact time when the star had appeared. Then he sent them to Bethlehem, saying, "Go and search diligently for the child; and when you have found him, bring me word so that I may also go and pay him homage." When they had heard the king, they set out; and there, ahead of them, went the star that they had seen at its rising, until it stopped over the place where the child was. When they saw that the star had stopped, they were overwhelmed with joy. On entering the house, they saw the child with Mary his mother; and they knelt down and paid him homage. Then, opening their treasure chests, they offered him gifts of gold, frankincense, and myrrh. And having been warned in a dream not to return to Herod, they left for their own country by another road.

I've always been intrigued by the wise men, and, at times, identified with them. Even in high school, I was destined to be a wise man. In the opera, *Amahl and the Night Visitors*, I was given the part of Kaspar. I actually played the part of one of these visitors from the East! In fact, for much of my life I have been called a wise man. Well, perhaps not exactly that. Maybe not so much a wise man, as a *wise guy*. But at least for an hour in high school I was truly a wise man.

In the movie, *Butch Cassidy and the Sundance Kid*, Butch and Sundance are trying to escape after a bank robbery, but a posse is coming after them. Every time Butch and Sundance stop and look back, no matter how they try to throw them off, the posse is still on their trail. Finally Butch turns to Sundance and asks, "Who are those guys"?

"Who are those guys?" This is the question that has been asked for centuries about the wise men. Who are they? What did they do? Where did they come from? What happened to them after they visited the Christ child?

Who are they? I wish I could tell you with great accuracy. I can tell you that wise men are based on the word "magi," and that there were magi all over that part of the world, especially in Persia. Most of the translations today translate magi as "wise men." But a few, including Moffatt, translate magi as "magicians."[1] I don't find this translation helpful. I can't imagine magicians being invited to visit the Christ child. That doesn't fit the Christmas setting. Jesus' birth is no sleight of hand; no smoke and mirrors. It is real and earthy in spite of its miraculous nature. I side with sources that suggest that these wise men were scholars—probably astrologers of some sort. They certainly did study the stars—we know that from the text. They could have even been from the priestly class. They may have been from Persia. We don't know. We do know with certainty that they were foreigners; that they came from afar. [2]

Wise men. Who were they? It is interesting that the two groups that God invites to the birth of his Son are so totally different. We have the shepherds on the one hand from Luke's gospel, and in Matthew's gospel we have the wise men. In reality they are both outsiders. But they are different types of outsiders. Let's contrast them.

The wise men are intelligent, learned, and well-heeled. The shepherds are—to be polite—less learned, less intelligent, and most certainly poor. The wise men are esteemed within their own culture. They have a certain status. The shepherds are low on the social ladder. The wise men are the foreigners. The shepherds are the local yokels, yet still not a part of the inner circle. There is a great deal of contrast between these two, but they have one inescapable thing in common: they are both outsiders. No one would have expected either of them to be invited to the birth of the Messiah.

The storyline of the two groups is different as well. In Luke's gospel, the shepherds get clear instructions. A reliable source, an angel, tells the shepherds about Jesus' birth and gives them specific directions. When the shepherds arrive, it is as they have been told. They encounter the Christ Child. They are transformed, no longer lowly shepherds, but believing evangelists. They return home to share the good news.

Matthew's magi have a much different experience. They are not given a clear mission nor are they given detailed directions—only to follow a star. They have to draw from their own knowledge and understanding if they are to find the Christ child. They will need dreams, discernment, and God's guidance if they are to be successful. It will not be a short trip like that of the shepherds, but rather a long arduous journey. Faith will be required of these outsiders, who have only a partial knowledge of the Scriptures.

When they see the star, the wise men decide to follow its light. To reach their goal, however, they will have to be adventurous. Another difference between the wise men and the shepherds is that the wise men have to settle for delayed gratification—the babe is not just over a few hills. I'm sure somewhere along the journey, the wise men must have said, "Are we crazy or what? Is this really going to happen; are we going to find the King of the Jews?" But they made that difficult journey anyway. When they arrived, the Christ child was no longer in a stable but a house. Unlike the portrayal of most nativity scenes, the wise men did not share the company of stable animals and visiting shepherds.

Of course most of us envision the nativity like those portrayed by artists. But the text says a *house*, and that should not be surprising. Mary and Joseph could not keep baby Jesus in a stable forever, could they? When the wise men finally arrive, they worship the Christ child just as the shepherds had worshipped before them.

We don't know whether or not these foreigners were transformed by their encounter with the Christ child. We do know that they immediately worshipped him. At the end of the story, the text says, "They left for their own country by another road." The Revised Standard Version says, "by another way." I like the unintentional double meaning in such language. It is quite possible that once the magi encountered the Christ child, they were transformed. They could not simply go back the way they had come. They would go home another way. They would go home transformed.

We learn nothing about the wise men after that. That is the end of the story. Not surprisingly, tradition has embellished the account through the years. It is human nature to do such. We tend to either etch ideas in stone or constantly fill in more details. Tradition has chosen to embellish this story of the wise men, these magi. So we now have several traditions that have developed over hundreds of years to the point that one might have these visitors from the East sing boldly, "We three kings of Orient are."

Perhaps not. We are certainly not sure about three. This is only conjecture. The biblical texts do not say "three." All we know for sure is that these foreigners brought three gifts for the Christ Child: gold, frankincense, and myrrh. Maybe there were two travelers, and they got together and bought three gifts. Or maybe it was a group of five magi that pooled their funds together and all they could buy were three lavish gifts. We don't know, but *three* wise men is not necessarily correct.

Kings? Probably not—even with all the tradition of great hymns and anthems and works of art. Can you imagine three separate kings ever agreeing on a single course of action or setting off on a long journey by themselves? Can you imagine three kings knowing enough about the stars to discern that something special was about to happen?

But kings do have a biblical basis. We find in Psalms 72:10–11 and in Isaiah 60:3 accounts about kings visiting from afar. Isaiah 60:6 even mentions gold and frankincense. But according to Matthew, these magi are not kings. Only by combining different biblical traditions can one refer to the wise men as kings. Still most nativity scenes reflect these visitors from the East as real kings complete with crowns and regal robes.

But of all the characteristics and descriptions that one could give of the wise men, there is one that is most central to the story: they were inescapably foreigners. They were foreigners in every sense: in culture, in geography, in religion. In other words, they were total outsiders. This story of the visit of the wise men becomes a story about outsiders being invited to become insiders.

These magi go to King Herod and to the real insiders, the chief priests and scribes, and ask about the birth of a Savior. The insiders know the answer. They share it with the outsiders who should not even care: "Yes, the King of the Jews is born in Bethlehem." Ironically, the insiders stay, and the outsiders go. The religious people blatantly ignore the coming of Christ, and those outside the religion eagerly trudge on to Bethlehem. The religious have the scriptures; they have the inside scoop; but they ignore it all. It is the foreigners who take the journey, who take the risk. They alone experience both the inside story and the rest of the story.

It is interesting to look at nativity scenes from other countries and other cultures. Some Americans may be surprised by the nativity scenes from Asia, at least the ones not meant for sale in United States. How is the Christ child portrayed? Asian! If one travels to Africa, guess what color baby Jesus will be? Black!

What is it that makes people want to envision the Christ child in their own image? Is it because they want to feel that the Christ child came to them? Or is it to declare themselves *insiders* and make all others *outsiders*? One thing is clear in the biblical account—it is the outsiders who become insiders. The Christmas story is clearly not about insiders who can thereby exclude others. The God of the New Testament is, in fact, the God of all the nations. The New Testament God is a God of both insiders and outsiders. The Messiah who comes will be a "light to the Gentiles and the people Israel." Any effort to make Jesus the exclusive possession of one culture is in direct conflict with the story of the magi from a foreign land.

But before we leave the theme of three kings, I would like to suggest a different number—and different kings for that matter. I would argue that the story of the nativity is not about three kings at all but only two kings—King Herod and King Jesus. The story is about choosing between the two and their kingdoms.

On the one hand, we have King Herod who has all the earthly power one can imagine yet is terrified at the birth of a tiny baby. On the other hand, we have Jesus, God coming among us in the most vulnerable way possible, in the form of a child.

There are two kings—King Herod and King Jesus. The wise men have one major decision to make. They have to discern which king to follow. Which one will they hear, and which one will they heed? They do make the right choice, by the way. They choose the king with the spiritual power over the one with the worldly power. They choose King Jesus.

The wise men become people of faith even though they have few trappings of religion. They make their journey and encounter the Christ child. What happens after that? Though we do not know, I choose to believe that they were transformed. I choose to believe that the wise men sought and the wise men found. I believe they went home a different way and as different people.

Many years ago I read a poignant saying on a Christmas card. Its words are absolutely true: "The wise still seek Jesus and the wise still find him, but the wisest of all follow him." This

Christmas, honoring those risk-taking magi, I would like to suggest a slightly different saying:
"Those who seek to be wise, truly wise,
    will no longer follow the light of a star.
        They will follow the Light of the world!"

Excerpt from
Christmas Journeys: Finding Joy along the Way by Dr. Justin Tull

NOTES

1. James A. R. Moffatt, *The Bible: James Moffatt Translation* (San Francisco: Harper Collins, 1955)
2. George Arthur Buttrick, ed., *The Interpreter's Dictionary of the Bible* (Nashville: Abingdon Press, 1962), p. 222.

Sermon Overview

Sermon Sentence: *The wise men were truly outsiders who became insiders; our goal is to do the same.*

Context: No significant event going on in the church

Category of Sermon: *Exegetical* (A portrayal of biblical characters using imagination and biblical research.)
Part of a series, "Faces of the Nativity"

Sermon Form: *Expanded narrative of the biblical account*
(Direct application for today reserved for the very end.)

Techniques: Humor, creativity, biblical research.

Purpose: To make the wise men real human beings rather than clay or glass figures in nativity scenes. To open up the congregation to the world of the *outsider.*

Ending: Leaving the story of the wise men, and turning to focus on the child they had journeyed to see.

General comments

This was part of a series entitled "Faces of the Nativity," given during the Sundays of Advent. The series included an expanded portrayal of Mary, Joseph, the shepherds, and the wise men. It allowed the congregation to see these biblical characters as truly human and deserving of our admiration and respect.

The Birthright Blues!

Genesis 25:19-34

These are the descendents of Isaac, Abraham's son: Abraham was the father of Isaac, and Isaac was forty years old when he married Rebekah, daughter of Bethuel the Aramean of Paddanaram, sister of Laban the Aramean. Isaac prayed to the Lord for his wife, because she was barren, and the Lord granted his prayer, and his wife Rebekah conceived. The children struggled together within her; and she said, "If it is to be this way, why do I live?" So she went to inquire of the Lord. And the Lord said to her, "Two nations are in your womb, and two peoples born of you shall be divided; the one shall be stronger than the other, the elder shall serve the younger." When her time to give birth was at hand, there were twins in her womb. The first came out red, all his body like a hairy mantle; so they named him Esau. Afterward his brother came out, with his hand gripping Esau's heel; so he was named Jacob. Isaac was sixty years old when she bore them.

When the boys grew up, Esau was a skillful hunter, a man of the field, while Jacob was a quiet man, living in the tents. Isaac loved Esau, because he was fond of game; but Rebekah loved Jacob.

Once when Jacob was cooking a stew, Esau came in from the field, and he was famished. Esau said to Jacob, "Let me eat some of that red stuff, for I am famished!" (Therefore he was called Edom.) Jacob said, "First sell me your birthright. Esau said, "I am about to die; of what use is a birthright to me?" Jacob said, "Swear to me first." So he swore to him, and sold his birthright to Jacob. Then Jacob gave Esau bread and lentil stew, and he ate and drank, and rose and went his way. Thus Esau despised his birthright.

D o you have the "birthright blues? Jane does. Listen to her story:

Jane: I am so plain and dull that I never have any dates.
Friend: Why don't you go to a good beauty salon and get a different hairdo?
Jane: Yes, but that costs too much money.
Friend: Well, how about buying a magazine with some suggestions for different ways of setting it yourself?
Jane: Yes, I tried that – and my hair is too fine. It doesn't hold a set. If I wear it in a bun, it at least looks neat.
Friend: How about using makeup to dramatize your features, then?
Jane: Yes, but my skin is allergic to makeup. I tried it once and my skin got rough and broke out.
Friend: They have lots of good, non-allergenic makeups out now. Why don't you go see a dermatologist?
Jane: Yes, but I know what he'll say. He'll say I don't eat right. I know I eat too much junk and don't have well-balanced meals. That's the way it is when you live by yourself. Oh, well, beauty is only skin deep.
Friend: Well, that's true. Maybe it would help if you took some adult education courses, like in art or current events. It helps make you a good conversationalist, you know.
Jane: Yes, but they're all at night. And after work I'm so exhausted.
Friend: Well, take some correspondence courses, then.
Jane: Yes, but I don't even have time to write letters to my folks. How could I ever find time for correspondence courses?
Friend: You could find time if it were important enough.
Jane: Yes, but that's easy for you to say. You have so much energy. I'm always so tired.
Friend: Why don't you go to bed at night? No wonder you're tired when you sit up and watch "The Late Show" every night.
Jane: Yes, but I've got to do something fun. That's all there is to do when you're like me! [1]

Have you ever met Jane? Have you ever sung her song? Tell me straight: "Do you have the 'birthright blues'?"

In our text for this morning there are many themes worth exploring. One could talk about sibling rivalry, Mama's boy versus Daddy's boy, macho versus cultured, brawn versus brain. But there is one theme that dominates the story and it concerns Esau's birthright. Why did he give it up so easily?

But first let me say a word about the birthright itself. In the Hebrew tradition, a birthright was really the right of the first-born son. It included holding "a position of honor as head of the family and a double share of the inheritance." [2]   In this particular case, one would assume it also meant inheriting the promise made to Abraham of a great nation and of a new land.

So this was no small thing that Esau traded away in a matter of minutes – and all for a bowl of lentils! Why did he do so? The easy answer is that he was just stupid. He did not understand the value of the birthright and so he was easily tricked out of it by a cunning younger brother.

One might also assume that Esau was one who lived only for the present moment. To him, "a bird in the hand" was always worth "two in the bush," or in this case, a "bowl in the hand" was surely worth "a birthright in the bush."

Perhaps one could even make the case that Esau was a modernist after all. He must have heard the '60's saying, "If it feels good, do it," and made his own adaptation: "If it looks good, trade for it."

But the last verse of our story suggests that none of these views reflect Esau's primary problem. Verse 34b gives our answer: "Thus Esau despised his birthright." Like our poor little Jane, Esau suffered from the "birthright blues." He did not treasure what he had been given. He was indifferent about it. He would trade it for anything, even the mushy contents of a bowl! To Esau it was worth nothing!

Esau suffered from the "birthright blues," and from that time forward thousands have followed his example. How far will the epidemic spread? It is hard to say. There are so many cases, even today. Are you one of them? Do you hate your birthright?

Do you feel gypped? Do your resent the body you received, your face, your intelligence, your lack of intelligence, your background, your inheritance, your lack of inheritance?

Jesus evidently was aware of the "birthright blues" syndrome. He even dedicated an entire parable to speak to it. You do remember the story about the talents, don't you? The master called his servants together and to one he gave five talents, to another, two, and to another, one. When he returned to receive back the money he had entrusted to them, the ones with two and five talents had used them wisely and doubled their worth, but the one who had only one talent had buried it in the ground.

If you ask me, he had a bad case of the "birthright blues." He was ashamed of what had been given to him. He treated it as if it had little value at all. The master was very angry with this ungrateful servant!

But I have to admit, it is very easy to slip into those "birthright blues." It is very easy to feel sorry for oneself. It is very easy to find others who receive "more" or "better."

So when we stand next to someone with a better body, a better brain, a prettier face, why not succumb to a little "birthright blues?" And why not follow Esau's example? Why not misuse what we have been given? Why not settle for the moment instead of waiting for a future payoff? Why not take something that God gave as special and treat it as though it were worth nothing?

And why should we ever care about the larger picture. Who cares about intended use? Why should we respect our birthright? Are we not free to do with our birthright as we choose? What we have is for our own use or abuse. Am I right?

The ultimate trap is to end up with no birthright at all, feeling that we have no promise from God and nothing to do.

So we bury our talent, sell our birthright and join Jane in our pitiful lament: "That's all there is to do when you're like (us)."

But the Bible says otherwise. It tells us to pick up our pallet of self-pity and walk. It tells us to "Go and sin no more." It tells us to welcome the stranger, care for the outcast. It tells us to love our neighbor as ourselves. It tells us to use all that we have for the glory of God, to let our lights shine.

Fortunately, there is an alternative to the "birthright blues." Ask Helen Keller, if anyone could get my vote as the most likely candidate for the "birthright blues," it would be Helen. Losing her sight and hearing before the age of two, she eventually made the journey from self-pity to communication and on to spirituality and love. I challenge any of us to place our self-pity next to hers and feel justified about our moodiness!

Tim Hansel said it right when he wrote, "Pain is inevitable, but misery is optional." [3] The "birthright blues" is a choice. It is not a given!

Perhaps some of you are afraid you will leave the service today without a reverent word. You are not a "plain Jane" or a talent waster. You have no "Cinderella" or "Cinderfella" complex. You do not feel short changed, but rather blessed. So where is your example if not Esau or Jacob?

You might try emulating the servants with the two and five talents by taking what has been given you and using it wisely, not for your own advancement, but for the sake of the Master who entrusted it to you.

The choice we make in life often is between two major options: living as though we have the "birthright blues" or the "birthday bonanza." Most of us feel one way or the other; either basically blessed with what we have been given or basically short changed.

This human dilemma is why this Old Testament lesson is so important to us and so relevant. It asks us if we join Esau in hating our birthright. It asks us if we are willing to settle for the moment, if we treat cheaply what has great value, if we pity ourselves when we have been given much.

So where are you right now? Are you slipping into the "birthright blues?" Are you celebrating your "birthday bonanza?"

And regardless of where you are right now, where do you want to be? Does Esau's route sound okay? Sell out cheap; hate what is yours.

What do you want to do with your talents? Put them alongside others and weep? Put them next to need, and serve?

What will be your basic stance in life? Gratitude or dissatisfaction?

So what will it be for you? Will you cast your pearls before swine, sell your birthright for a cup of chili, bury your talent or use it, be grateful for all that has been given to you or pout in the corner until you win the lottery?

Will you live only for the moment, care more about food and money than meaning and purpose, value life or devalue it?

Let me make it simple for now: What will your autobiography be titled: *Birthright Blues* or *Birthday Bonanza?* You decide!

Excerpt from *Wrestlings, Wonders, and Wanderers* by Dr. Justin Tull

NOTES

1. Thomas A. Harris, M.D., I'm O.K., You're O.K., A Practical Guide to Transactional Analysis (New York: Harper and Row, Publishers, 1967), pp. 120-121.
2. Cuthbert A. Simpson, *Genesis, vol. 1 of The Interpreter's Bible*, ed. George Arthur Buttrick (New York: Abingdon Press, 1952), p. 668.
3. Tim Hansel, *You Gotta Keep Dancin'* (Elgin, Illinois: David C. Cook Publishing Co., 1985), p. 35.

SERMON OVERVIEW

Sermon Sentence: *Accept the talents that God has given you and use them to bless others and yourself.*

Context: No specific church issues were addressed.

Category of Sermon: *Existential*
(How can we value what God has given us?)

Sermon Form: *Repetition of a Theme ("Birthright Blues")*
Today/ Biblical times/ Today

Techniques: Storytelling, humor, biblical research, drama, imagination, closing question

Purpose: To encourage the listeners to accept their birthright and see their life as blessed

Ending: A question demanding the listener to choose between two life scripts: one of gratitude or one of disdain.

GENERAL COMMENTS

This sermon was an invitation for every listener to first determine his or her life stance. Did they feel blessed by all they had been given or short changed? Hopefully, those who might feel cheated by life will reconsider in light of the sermon's narrative.

The Parable of the Talents Revisited!

Matthew 25:14-30

For it is as if a man, going on a journey, summoned his slaves and entrusted his property to them; to one he gave five talents, to another two, to another one, to each according to his ability. Then he went away. The one who had received the five talents went off at once and traded with them, and made five more talents. In the same way, the one who had the two talents made two more talents. But the one who had received the one talent went off and dug a hole in the ground and hid his master's money. After a long time the master of those slaves came and settled accounts with them. Then the one who had received the five talents came forward, bringing five more talents, saying, 'Master, you handed over to me five talents; see, I have made five more talents.' His master said to him, 'Well done, good and trustworthy slave; you have been trustworthy in a few things, I will put you in charge of many things; enter into the joy of your master.' And the one with the two talents also came forward, saying, 'Master, you handed over to me two talents; see, I have made two more talents.' His master said to him, 'Well done, good and trustworthy slave; you have been trustworthy in a few things, I will put you in charge of many things; enter into the joy of your master.' Then the one who had received the one talent also came forward, saying, 'Master, I knew that you were a harsh man, reaping where you did not sow, and gathering where you did not scatter seed; so I was afraid, and I went and hid your talent in the ground. Here you have what is yours.' [26] But his master replied, 'you wicked and lazy slave! You knew, did you, that I reap where I did not sow, and gather where I did not scatter? Then you ought to have invested my money with the bankers, and on my return I would have received what was my own with interest. So take the talent from him, and give it to the one with the ten talents. For to all those who have, more will be given, and they will have an abundance; but from those who have nothing, even what they have will be taken away. As for this worthless slave, throw him into the outer darkness, where there will be weeping and gnashing of teeth.'

The Great Creator God called four of his creatures to the Great Hall. It was the twenty-first birthday for all of them: Eric, Joe, Ann, and Tiffany. And the Creator said to them:

I have decided to give out eighteen talents to you today. You will not receive an equal number. The most you can receive is ten and the least is one. This is not the lottery. It is not by chance that you receive what you receive. Use these talents wisely for the good of all and always treat them as a gift… Eric, please come forward.

Eric received an envelope from the Creator. He hurriedly opened it and immediately yelled out, "Ten! Yes!" He looked back at the others who were staring at him, dropped his gaze down at his feet and slipped the envelope in his front pocket.

Joe, please come forward.

Joe took his envelop and opened it very slowly. He stepped backwards a few steps and then managed a faint, "Thanks," before returning to the group.

Ann!

On her way to her Maker, Ann saw Joe's card sticking out of his pocket. She could make out the large number—"TWO." *That makes twelve,* Ann thought to herself. *That means there are only six left.* As Ann continued her short walk to the Creator God, she wondered how many talents she would get.

The Creator did not give the envelope to Ann as soon as she stood before him. Instead, the Creator addressed her directly, *"Use all these talents well, and never be ashamed of any of them."*

Ann bowed slightly as she took her envelope. She opened it on her way back. She couldn't believe it—she got five talents! She could have gotten one or two or perhaps three, but she got five of the last six talents. When Ann returned to the foursome, Tiffany seemed to be reading her face. The expression of "wonderful surprise" gave Tiffany little hope for her chances.

And last, but not least, Tiffany!

Tiffany went forward slowly and timidly reached out her hand. The Creator God placed the envelope firmly in Tiffany's hand and smiled. The envelope looked exactly like the others, plain and white with nothing written on the outside. But when she opened the envelope, Tiffany was surprised with what she found—a beautifully textured white card with an elaborate gold embossed number—"ONE." But in this case it did not mean *being* number one. It stood for *last,* and *least.*

Tiffany's face reflected her number all too well. She swallowed hard but managed to respond to her gift. "Thank you God," she said and walked back to the group. Then the Creator God turned to the four of them, now raising his voice so they could hear clearly.

> *You have been given one or more talents—all of a different variety. You will each be tempted to misuse your talents. They are different temptations, but temptations none the less. Guard against them. Use wisely everything I have given you and remember, "It is a gift." Consider it a "birthday" gift if you wish. I have planned a special party for the four of you on the occasion of your fiftieth birthday. There will be many guests here to welcome you. If will be a time of reporting back, if you know what I mean. I will send a limo to pick you up and bring you to the Great Hall. Until then… Peace be with you.*

Eric, Ann, Joe, and Tiffany walked outside, not speaking to one another. It was so incredibly awkward. What could anyone say? Finally Ann broke the silence. "Well, I guess I'll see you all back here for our fiftieth!" The three others quickly echoed back, "See you at the fiftieth!"

The next twenty-nine years had much in store for each of them…

Eric wasted no time at all. He discovered he could make lots of money with his number one talent—athletic ability. He became a super-star. He was a great athlete and did not lack for flair! Jay Leno once asked him the secret of his success. "Just working hard and always doing my best!" he said with great pride. But the truth was, Eric rarely did his best. He was often satisfied with about seventy percent. Why do your best when with a little effort you can still be very good? Why really work hard for excellence when being good comes so easily?

As the years went by, Eric forgot all about his twenty-first birthday at the Great Hall. He forgot about the card with the large number ten embossed on it. Eric had learned by now that life does not *bestow* gifts. If you want them, you just have to *take* them. Eric once yelled at his agent over the phone, "You tell them I'm not going to work for peanuts! I'm a super star!" Eric had mastered the art of the *dynamic duo* of *coastin'* and *boastin'*.

Joe did not do as well as Eric. Joe certainly had no big income or fame. In fact, Joe had a problem just keeping a job. Oh, he had ability to make it in the work force. It was Joe's attitude that caused the problems. He had trouble getting along with anyone who had a better job or bigger salary. Joe saw himself as a *nobody*. Everybody else seemed to have so much more than he did.

Joe was always angry, but I'm not sure he realized why. If the truth were known, Joe was angry at the Creator for short-changing him. Joe knew he was just as good as Eric, but Eric got ten talents and he got two. Eric got all the breaks, all the fame, all the money—even a fantastic looking wife. It wasn't fair.

Joe was so wrapped up in himself that it never occurred to him that he might not have gotten the least number of talents. He assumed that Ann and Tiffany had gotten three each leaving him with the lowest haul of only two. Joe treated himself not as a number two, not as a silver medalist, but as *dead last*—and I do mean *dead*. Joe had chosen as his life's work the *manufacturing and distribution of pity and anger*."

Meanwhile Ann had done fairly well using her talents. She was now a successful business woman. She started a non-profit for battered women and managed a thrift store that helped support her annual budget. She had suffered abuse herself in her first marriage. Now she was trying to help others who had fallen victim like herself.

Ann had to grow into full use of her talents. It was in her work with the non-profit that Ann finally managed to use all five. For some time she had carried around two talents she rarely used. Finally, she dusted them off and began using them in her work. It paid off. She won a grant from a large foundation for her non-profit. Who would have thought that a winsome personality and problem solving skills could be such a powerful combination?

It had not been an easy road for Ann. Remember those words of the Creator, words about temptations that would come to each recipient? Ann certainly knew what her temptation was. Even though she received far more talent that either Joe or Tiffany, Ann could0000n't help comparing herself to Eric. In spite of all she had been given—more than most others—she was still jealous and envious!

It was during her painful divorce that Ann changed her philosophy of life. Her talents had enabled her to survive. They helped her salvage her self-esteem. As Ann put her life back together, she decided to use her gifts not just for herself. She decided to dedicate them for a greater cause, a higher purpose.

Ann was happy now—happier than she had been before her marriage went sour, happier than on her twenty-first birthday when she got five out of the last six talents. Ann now knew her life was blessed. She needed nothing more.

One day Tiffany entered Ann's thrift store. She was there picking out clothes for a job interview. She had managed to get her G.E.D. and finally had her own apartment. Things had been on the upswing until losing her job several weeks back.

Finally Ann saw Tiffany across the room—at least she thought it was Tiffany. After watching for a while Ann approached her

Excuse, me, but aren't you Tiffany?

Yes, and you're Ann, right? I'm just curious. How many talents did you get?

I got five—but I feel badly for you. I think there was only one talent left when you went up. That's what you got—one—right?

Yes.

Well didn't you resent getting just one? I would have.

Yes. I resented it for some time. I was a bit jealous of all of you. I was even jealous of Joe. I saw his card. He got twice as many as I got. You know, it's strange how life works. It's strange how sadness can sometimes lead to happiness—how bad news can become good news.

I think I know what you mean. But tell me more.

I got fired a couple of weeks ago and I was ready to throw in the towel. I thought about doing something bad to myself. I was angry and hurting and sad. Life was just not fair. I had gotten the short end of the stick and it all started at the Great Hall.

But for some reason the Creator's words came back to me. Do you remember what he said? He said, "This is not the lottery!" That means he gave me the one talent on purpose, just as he gave you five talents. I don't know why He did that, but I accept it now.

I've decided to do what he asked us to do—to take what we've been given and use it wisely. Hey, I've got the easiest job. I just have to use one talent. You have to use four more!

Listen. I better be going. I need to get back home.

Sure. Do you want to check out?

Ann thought about maybe giving Tiffany the clothes but she took the money and gave her the change. They both smiled and said goodbye.

Ann watched tiffany leave the store with a sack of clothes under her arm. Ann prayed a simple prayer that Tiffany would get the job. But as she said "Amen," a thought flashed into her mind. She dashed out the door and hurried over to where Tiffany was waiting on the bus.

Tiffany, if you don't get the job, let me know. I think I might have something for you at the store.
Thanks, Ann. That's nice, but I think I'll get it. See you at the fiftieth.
See you at the fiftieth!

The big night finally arrived. The Great Hall was decorated to the hilt. A giant number fifty towered at the far end of the room. There was the "tacky corner" with black balloons and the words "Over the Hill!" There was the "affirming corner" with the words, "the best is yet to be." And the "nostalgic corner" with photographs of the twenty-first birthday party with Eric, Joe, Ann, and Tiffany. The photographer had captured perfectly their expressions as they opened their envelopes: jubilation, disappointment, relief, resignation. The fourth corner was blank except for a large sticky note that read, "To be filled in later."

There were hundreds of people gathered for the formal banquet. Past recipients had been invited back. At the middle of the head table was Eric sitting next to the Creator of All. Other special guests were also present. Ann was seated at the far end of the head table. Joe was seated at a table just below the platform. Tiffany was near the back. She was talking to the waitress who had just served her the salad.

The Creator stood and welcomed all his guests.

> *Twenty-nine years ago four people here were given wonderful talents. Tonight is a time of accountability. Tonight inequality will become equal and unfairness, right.*

> *Eric Grandiose is on my right. Eric did not use well the talents I gave him. He used only one of the ten talents and that is the one which could benefit him the most. Quite often he put out only minimum effort,*

settling for good when he could have achieved excellence. Worst of all, he forgot that the successes he enjoyed were not the result of his own greatness, but only possible because of the gifts I gave him.

I have cancelled his contracts and assigned him as the head fitness coach for the Johnson Fitness Center that serves children with special needs. I hope they will be an inspiration to him. Eric, I will allow you to keep your athletic talent since you did use it, but the rest of the nine I will have to take back.

Eric sat down. But this time, no swagger in his movement—no smirk on his face. He stared down at his plate as the Great God called out the next name.

Ann, you had your struggles, didn't you? It's tough to be good when you want to be the best, isn't it? I'm glad you have learned what "outstanding" really means! I'm proud of all your struggles. Oh by the way, that was a nice gesture offering the job to Tiffany. But you don't feel sorry for her any more, do you?

Ann shook her head, "no," not daring to speak.

I thought about giving you more talents, I think I'll stick with five. Continue using them creatively. Never forget that they are both a gift and a responsibility! You have done well.

Without a pause the Great God looked down upon a figure sitting in front of him. Neither looked pleased at that moment.

Joe, you are the greatest disappointment of all! I gave you two perfectly good talents and you refused to use either of them. You have been consumed by jealousy and self-pity. So, since you never used your talents, I'm taking them back. And don't you dare feel cheated, unless, that is, you finally realize you cheated yourself! I'll see you back here on your sixtieth birthday. Maybe by then you will be able to recognize a gift when you see it.

The Great God's countenance suddenly changed; it became softer and kinder, like a proud parent gazing at a sleeping child.

Tiffany, dear Tiffany, you did not disappoint me. You fought the hard battle with resentment and self-pity, and won. You listened to my voice inside your head. You used every bit of the talent I gave you. And you did it with a gracious spirit, with a kind heart.

You may not need any more talents, but I'm giving you these nine that Eric refused to use. You can use them for yourself or give them away. Come. Receive my embrace and take these new gifts for yourself!

Tiffany walked hurriedly to the head table and stood timidly before the Creator God.

Tiffany, perhaps you would like to say a word, to all our guests?

Tiffany pulled the microphone close to her lips and took a deep breath before she spoke. "*I am grateful for life. I am grateful for the talent I was given. I am truly blessed!*"

The Creator God embraced Tiffany fondly and then nodded as a cue for her dismissal. As Tiffany made her way, she stopped where Joe was sitting. She pulled a one talent card from an envelope and handed it to him. *One is all you need, Joe, if you treat it like a gift. See you at the sixtieth!*"

As Tiffany made her way to her seat, Eric, in his first ever sign of humility, stood up and began to clap. Before Tiffany reached her place the entire audience was standing and applauding. They were paying tribute to one of the greatest among them. Then the Great Creator God stood and addressed all the assembly.

I have given each of you talents and abilities. It is not by chance that you have them. I know their names and I know their number. Use them wisely and for the benefit of others—like Tiffany and Ann have. If you do, you will discover the special joy of each gift!

My blessing rests upon you all! See you at your sixtieth!

And the crowd all responded...

SERMON OVERVIEW

Sermon Sentence: *God calls us to use all our gifts wisely, treating them as gifts, and sharing their blessing with others.*

Context: No urgent Church need was addressed

Category of Sermon: *Existential Dilemma*
(What to I do with   my gifts?)

Sermon Form: A creative narrative expanding the scope of the parable.

Techniques Used: Composing a narrative not only to make a point, but also to draw in the congregation through the power of identification.

Purpose: To invite everyone present to consider how they have used their talents and to offer hope that they might change the way they use their gifts for the better.

Ending: Ending turned away from the story and addressed the listener directly, challenging them to use their own talents and reminding them of accountability. The refrain of "See you at the sixtieth" (Which, hopefully, the congregation echoed out loud) was a reminder of that future accountability.

GENERAL COMMENTS

I love to compose sermons as one all-encompassing narrative. Unfortunately, they take about three times the amount of time to create. I have done no more than ten of these creations in my ministry. Most texts do not lend themselves to such a form. I have created many stories from my imagination, but they have served as only part of the sermon, not its entirety.

On this occasion I decided to do an expansion of the parable because the original parable does not include all the different scenarios of how one can use or misuse talent. Of course, I realized that "talent" was not originally a reference to abilities, but rather a form of currency. But the application of the parable to modern-day talents is both a logical adaption and one that is biblically justified.

In the parable, the servants with the most talents use them wisely and the servant with the one talent buries his in the ground. Certainly there are ample life stories of both scenarios—people with great talent who use it to the fullest and people with little talent who dig a hole big enough to bury their talent and themselves at the same time. But the thrust of the parable, its moral command, is that we are called to use all the talents we have, no matter how many, or how few.

The revised and expanded parable makes clear that the person with many talents may well waste them and that the person with few talents may also use them fully, shaming the rest of us for our mediocre effort.

Another new twist to this story is to suggest that the use of talents is not something that is decided once and then put on auto pilot—it has to be decided day after day. And it is not a mere function of action; attitude is at the very heart of the matter.

In creating the scenario I reverse the *winners* of the story. The hero of the expanded story is the one with almost nothing, reminding us that it is not how much talent we have that determines our worth, but only how well we use it.

I use the birthday celebrations to reflect the seasons of our lives and how with each passage of time, we are given an opportunity to squander or use fully our talents. Ann and Tiffany are on the right track. Joe and Eric still have time to wake up and start living, not for selfish advantage, but for the sake of others. Hopefully, the listener will understand that such transformation is possible even for them.

I have preached this sermon to my congregation and also in more "secular" settings. I was asked to give the homily for chapel at an Episcopal school—seventh grade through seniors. (What a challenge!) I decided that this sermon was one that would be very relevant for a group of teenagers.

I was only a minute into the story when a "hush" fell over the gathering. I had the absolute attention of everyone—students and teachers alike. Was it because it was such a great story? I don't think so—though the story form was certainly effective. It was captivating because every teenager in that room had struggled just like those four young adults. Everyone there had a person with whom to identify. Everyone there knew instinctively that talents and attitudes toward them are a huge factor in how we live our lives.

Hopefully, I gave the students pause to consider their own use of their abilities. Hopefully, they now will be kinder to the Tiffanys of their world. Hopefully, they will also be less impressed with the Erics who *strut their stuff* through the hallways.

Beyond a Genie Mentality of Prayer!

Matthew 7:7-11

Ask, and it will be given you; search, and you will find; knock, and the door will be opened to you. For everyone who asks receives, and everyone who searches finds, and for everyone who knocks, the door will be opened. Is there anyone among you who, if your child asks for bread, will give a stone? Or if the child asks for a fish, will give a snake? If you then, who are evil, know how to give good gifts to your children, how much more will your Father in heaven give good things to those who ask them!

The scripture says, "Ask and it will be given you." Do any of any of you really believe that? Always? Has it worked for you?

My first wife and I owned a cabin in southern Colorado. It was first owned by my wife's parents, but they later gave it to us. Now the upkeep was our responsibility, and this particular summer we were going to have to spend most of our time there—not relaxing and hiking and resting—but scraping and painting the cabin.

My father-in-law called about two weeks before our trip to tell us about a strange and wonderful thing that happened to him. I listened as he broke the good news to me.

Justin, you know that storage shed out back? Well, I was cleaning it to help you out and I discovered some old glass milk bottles—you know, the ones that bulge out at the top for the cream. Well, anyway, as I picked up one of the bottles and rubbed the dirt off of it, a genie popped out!

A genie? I said.

Yeah, a real live Genie—not a super big one—but a genie, none-the-less. He turned to me and said, "You have one wish!" I told him I thought you get three wishes, but he wasn't budging. "One wish, and make it quick!" He said.

What did you ask for?

Son, I asked that you and Lynn would not have to paint the cabin this summer.

Would you believe, when I got to Colorado and turned the corner and looked up at the cabin, it was beautiful; it had a fresh coat of green paint. We would not be painting after all. Aren't genies great?

Fred Craddock is my favorite preacher of all times. He is a biblical scholar, a great teacher, and a super preacher. He tells the story of his first fall in Atlanta, Georgia. It's football season! Fred was invited to the game of the Georgia Bulldogs and he got to see Hershel Walker run the ball for the first time.

After the game—the bulldogs won by the way—the hostess invited everyone to their palatial home in Atlanta. She was dressed like she had just come from the opera, not a ballgame. As soon as she got everyone's attention she made an announcement. "I just want you to know—and I'm not ashamed to admit it—I prayed that our bulldogs would win and, praise God, they did."

Craddock said she then burst out singing in full voice the doxology: "Praise God from whom all blessings flow…"

I want you to know Fred Craddock is a very religious man. He has sung the doxology many times, but he just couldn't seem to get the words out that night. You see, Fred wasn't sure whether it was "Jesus" or the "running of Hershel Walker" that secured the victory.

I'm wondering, "Do you have a genie mentality of prayer?" "Ask and it will be given to you." Really?

When I went to my first church as pastor, I would often go to the local nursing home and visit from room to room. As I was making my rounds that day, a lady came up to me and said, "Are you a minister?" I wanted to say, "No, I'm the health inspector." But I said, "Yes."

I just want you to know I'm mad at God.

Why's that?

Well, I bought a new Cadillac six months ago and I have prayed every day that God would watch over it, and just last week someone ran into me and dented the front bumper. I'm mad at God.

In my first church I was associate pastor with responsibility for the youth program. I had several youth who became very religious. They witnessed to their friends at school. They read their Bibles every day and they prayed a lot.

One Sunday night several began witnessing about the power of prayer. A young teenage boy was the first to witness.

I was on my bike riding home and there was a storm cloud over my head. I did not want to get wet, so I prayed to God to prevent it from raining and not one drop fell on my head.

(I have to admit I did not like hearing this news because we were in a draught and needed the rain.) Not to be outdone, a young lady stood and told of her experience of the power of prayer:

> *It was during halftime and I was in the drill team at full attention when I realized I had a piece of chicken in my front teeth. I could not reach up so I just prayed to God and the morsel just fell to my tongue.*

Don't you love it when God can be as handy as dental floss? Do you have a genie mentality of prayer?

Not all the youth group had the same purpose for prayer. One of the youth focused his prayers on the health of his grandfather. Every day he would go by and visit his grandfather after school. Every night he would ask God to help his grandfather to get well, not to let him die. But his grandfather did die and this young man had a crisis of faith. He dropped out of the youth group. He had prayed to God believing God would spare his grandfather, but his grandfather died.

If we look at our text for today, we see implications that not everything we want will be granted. Jesus tells if we ask we will receive, but he also says sometimes we will have to search, sometimes we will have to knock—and there are no time limits for when these blessings will come.

Jesus also reasons that we will give good things to our own children. But let me ask you. "Will you give everything your child asks for?" Why not? Because everything they want is not necessarily good for them.

Several years ago I discovered one short verse in the book of James. Here is what James 4:3 tells us: "You ask and do not receive because you ask wrongly, in order to spend what you get on you pleasures."

(Oh, how I wish I had known that scripture when the lady with the busted bumper confronted me!)

If we look at the whole of scriptures not everyone gets what they ask for. Moses didn't get to see the promise land. Paul doesn't always get what he wants.

Paul, in his letter to the church at Corinth, complains about a thorn in his side. We don't know what it was really. It might have been epilepsy, or migraines or recurring malaria. Whatever it was, it was painful and Paul prayed that it be taken way. Listen to his words from 2 Corinthians 12:7-8:

> Therefore to keep me from being too elated, a thorn was given me in the flesh, a messenger of Satan to torment me, to keep me from being too elated. Three times I appealed to the Lord about this, that it would leave me, but he said to me, "My grace is sufficient."

Paul asked, but he did not receive. God did, however, answer Paul's prayer. He told Paul that God's grace would be enough. God would not change the circumstances of Paul's life, but instead would help him to live with those circumstances.

It is Jesus who told us, "ask and you will receive." How does his life reflect his understanding of prayer?

Do any of you remember Jesus' temptation in the wilderness? Remember, how Satan tempts Jesus who has been without food for forty days and forty nights? He tempts Jesus with food. What are Satan's words?

"If you are the Son of God, command that these stones become loaves of bread." Satan is saying "Ask and it will be given you."

But Jesus does not use his power to serve himself. He replies to Satan, "One does not live by bread alone, but by every word that comes from the mouth of God."

Jesus also gives us guidance for our praying with his model prayer for us—the Lord's Prayer. What does Jesus suggest we ask for?

Daily bread. Not filet mignon or red snapper. Not an evening out at our favorite restaurant.
Daily bread. Not just food but that which will sustain us.

What else are we to pray for?
"And forgive us our trespasses…"
Forgiveness. Yes, ask for forgiveness.

Anything else?
"And lead us not into temptation but deliver us from evil."
Ask for God's help in living each day.

But if we want Jesus' most powerful modeling of prayer we will find that in the Garden of Gethsemane. Jesus is now facing the reality of his imminent death. He does not want to die. He will lift his prayer request to his Father. "Father, if it is possible, let this cup pass from me…" And then he adds a most important condition for his request, "Yet not what I want but what you want." (Matthew 26:39b)

For Jesus, prayer was never simply a request line; it was a relationship. Jesus' praying was not about *his* wants and *his* wishes—these Jesus placed within the greater context of the "will of God!" "Nevertheless, not my will but thine be done." (KJV)

Do you have a genie mentality of prayer? Is prayer mainly a request line, getting God to do things for you?

You might ask, "Does God answer all prayers?" I think so. Sometimes that answer is "no." My young man in the youth group wanted his grandfather to keep on living, but his loved one died.

I prayed a lot when my wife had brain cancer. I don't think I ever asked that she be miraculously healed. Maybe that was because the doctors gave us no hope. But I did pray for quality of life. My wife lived much longer than all expected—not three months but twenty-seven months, and most of them were with a good quality of life—all but the last few. Looking back, God did answer my prayers. In a sense he answered them the same way he answered Paul. "My grace is sufficient." And it was!

Are there some prayers God always answers "yes."? I think so.
Will you please forgive me, God? "Yes"
Will you empower me to do your will? "Yes."
Will you be with me—even through the valley and shadow of death? "Absolutely!"

How do you understand prayer? What do you ask for?
      Please tell me you don't pray for parking spaces.
      Please tell me you don't just pray for your own needs.
What is prayer for you? A Request line? Or a relationship?

Many years ago I received a telephone call from my son during the end of his first semester. To be honest he didn't call much, so my wife and I were thrilled.

"Yes, we are doing fine."
> (Aside to my wife: "He's asking about us!")

After about ten minutes of conversation which was all very upbeat, there was suddenly a long pause. And then my son said, *"Oh, by the way…*

(Aside to the congregation; "You know what's coming!")
"Oh, by the way…
> I'm a little short on _____!"

That's right.   He could use a little *cash*.

Let me just say that my wife and I were still glad he called, but we were a bit disappointed because it seemed that the main reason he called was not to visit with us, to be in relationship, but simply to ask a favor.

I wonder if God ever feels that way about our prayers—glad we called, but disappointed because we mainly just want something.

How surprised and pleased God must be when we act differently. What if we ended our prayers another way?

Oh, by the way…
Oh, by the way… is there anything I can do for You?

SERMON OVERVIEW

Sermon Sentence: *Prayer is not a request line but a relationship that requires listening as well as speaking.*

Context: Two months after the tragic death of the senior pastor, many in the congregation were having a crisis of faith. You could almost hear their cries: "I prayed that my pastor might live. She died. How do I make sense of that? What can I expect from my prayer requests?"

Category of Sermon: *Theological* (What is prayer?)

Sermon Form: A series of stories and biblical texts to enlighten our understanding of prayer.

Techniques: Presenting false interpretations of prayer. Comparing these theologies to those of Paul and Jesus. Sharing a personal account of prayer in the face of death. Using the phoning home scenario to undermine selfish praying.

Purpose: To offer a new understanding of prayer to those having a crisis of faith, one grounded in a relationship rather than in wish fulfillment.

Ending: Building on the analogy of the phone call from a college student, I invited the listener to enter into God's world. How would God feel about our constant prayer requests? I invited those present to consider *listening* to God.

GENERAL COMMENTS

This sermon had early roots in my pastoral experience where youth, all excited about being religious, were misrepresenting the power and intent of prayer. This sermon set out to free prayer from being held hostage by requests, allowing instead for it to grow and mature. This sermon on prayer is a sermon for all places because it addresses a universal need, one central to our faith.

Hey! Where's My Gold Star?

Luke 17:7-10

"Will any one of you, who has a servant plowing or keeping sheep, say to him when he has come in from the field, 'Come at once and take your place at the table'?" Would you not rather say to him, 'Prepare supper for me, and gird yourself and serve me, 'til I eat and drink; and afterward you shall eat and drink'? Does he thank the servant because he did what was commanded? So you also when you have done all that is commanded you, say, 'We are unworthy servants; we have only done what was our duty.'" (RSV)

Do you have a favorite parable? Maybe the "Good Samaritan," or the "Prodigal Son," or the "Laborers in the Vineyard"?

Show of hands… Favorite Parable…
How many would pick the "Good Samaritan"?
How many of you would pick the "Prodigal Son"?
Anyone here for the "Laborers in the Vineyard"?
Any others?

And how many of you picked as your very favorite parable the one I read for you today? I thought so. It is not a very popular parable—it doesn't even have a name. Not many sermons are preached on this one.

Why is that? It's because we don't like the message. The parable suggests we should not expect reward for the good things we do. So what is the point of doing good then? That doesn't seem fair does it? Surely, we are not expected to do good for nothing!

One word of caution when applying a parable: you don't apply the "plot of the story" but rather look for the main message. Oftentimes a parable has one target group. In this parable Jesus isn't showing us how to treat those who work for us—expecting much from them and showing no appreciation.

He is talking about the attitude of the servants of the parable. They expect special treatment when they are only doing their jobs—what they are supposed to do. The parable is centered on the attitude of the servants, not the actions of the employer.

I have decided to label this attitude the "gold star syndrome." And we have all seen this attitude. We have even *had* this attitude from time to time.

I don't want to seem sexist, but I think in looking at the behavior of most husbands and most wives, I think maybe that men may have more trouble with this parable than women. Men are perhaps more likely to suffer from the "gold star syndrome."

I was told many times that before you get married you should check out the mother-in-law, that she will be the best clue as to how things might turn out. No one told me to look at the father-in-law. Boy, did I get blind-sided!

First, you have to know something about my own father. He was a very hard worker, owned his own shoe store, got up at five every morning, did all the house repairs, and raised a garden on the back lot. He worked all the time—except after meals. My Dad, in my memory, never took a glass or a plate to the sink. Never washed the dishes, never dried them. My Dad did men's work. He did not do "women's work."

147

Ironically, my mother did not accept that this practice should apply to her male children, so my brother and I washed and dried dishes, hung out clothes, ironed, vacuumed, cleaned. Anything that needed doing in the house, we did it. But my Dad? Nada.

Then I got married. One day I decided to wash the dishes after dinner. I finished and waited for my proper reward. I really didn't know if it would be a gushy "thank you," warm signs of affection, or what. I waited for my *gold star*, but all I got was a smile and a simple thank you. I expected much more for my generous efforts. When I pleaded my case, my wife only had to say, "My Dad did that all the time. You are *supposed* to help around the house."

At my church, a father brought his three young children to church each Sunday. The mother did not come. When word got out that he got them ready, fed them and brought them to worship, the older ladies of the church were ready to crown him father of the year. When I mentioned it to my wife she said, "Who does those things the other six days of the week?" I understood her point.

There is a good reason the gold star syndrome is alive and well. We parents have some responsibility for that. Want the kids to behave? Promise them a reward and then one day we realize we have created a monster. Our child looks up at us and declares, "I just picked up my toys, so you need to take me to McDonalds."

It's hard to undo a principle. How do we tell them that every good thing we do does not deserve a reward?

My daughter, when she was in the restaurant business, complained that some of her employees expected a bonus or praise—just for doing their job—some for just showing up for work. "It's their job!" she told me. "We pay them good wages. That's their reward."

I know of no better example of the *gold star syndrome* than in the arena of professional football. I can still vaguely remember, before all the cameras, when linemen would make a tackle and walk back to the defensive huddle. Now, when someone makes a tackle, they strut around and pound on their chests as if they have just done something unbelievable. I want to remind them that it is really their job as a defensive lineman to make tackles. In fact, we have probably paid him $10,000 dollars for the tackle.

Everywhere—at work, in the home, on the field—people expect to be rewarded for every good thing they do. They want their *gold star.* I want my *gold star?* Do you?

I took out the garbage, so I can take Saturday off to play golf, right?
I made good grades this semester, so I do get a car, don't I?

Oh, these scenarios can lead to serious attitude problems, but nothing compared to asking for *gold stars* from God.

Have you ever been good and expected God to bless you in some special way—I mean more than normal?

When something bad happens to us, do we turn to God and ask, "Why God why?" Aren't we really saying, "I've been good; I deserve blessings, not tragedy!"?

Jesus knew all about the *gold star syndrome*. In fact, I think those were the ones he was addressing in this parable—the people who expected God to reward them for their good behavior.

Do you remember the ones Jesus condemned the most? Remember those words, "Woe to you…"

Jesus condemned the *gold star* people—the ones who thought God owed them something because they had been so good, so religious.

The Scribes and Pharisees went about following the rules, but they were always expecting some kind of reward for their efforts. They thought doing good deserved special treatment from God. Even Job had made this mistake.

How many of us when we are good, expect a little extra from God? How many of us want a *gold star* from God?

This morning I want you to imagine heaven for a moment. Imagine my walking up to the pearly gates. (By the way, I am wearing around my neck a very large, very glittering gold star.) I meet a young man in dazzling apparel.

And who are you?
"Dr. Tull."
I'm sorry, we don't have titles here, but since you just got here, I'll call you "Just in."
Fine.
Well, "Just in," how may I help you?
I was wondering about my reward.
Oh, we don't use that word here. We do have words like "grace" and "blessing." but not "reward."
I mean, don't we get something, like maybe a golden crown?
Oh, a gold crown. Yes, I have yours and just your size.

150

Heaven was okay, I guess. I saw a few others walking around but I mostly kept to myself. None of the others wore their earthly gold stars, but all wore their crowns—which all looked alike. It bothered me at first that all the crowns were the same, none shinier than the others. I still wondered about my gold star. So I asked the one who greeted me at the gate.

"Could I see God sometime?" I asked.
I don't think that will be possible right now. Perhaps later.
I want to know why there are no gold stars up here.
That's something you will need to figure out on your own.

After a while I stopped wearing my star. I put it away under a tiny cloud. I started thinking about my life. I had always loved those gold stars. Now no one cared about them.

One day it finally dawned on me. There was *one* time in my life when I didn't care about gold stars. It was when my wife was critically ill with a brain tumor. I don't think there was ever a time I was a better father, a better husband or better minister than those twenty-seven months before her death. Yet I did not think about deserving a gold star—not for anything I was doing. I only did what I should have done. I only did what she would have done for me had the illness chosen me instead of her.

I remembered back to those words I spoke to her..."for richer, for poorer, in sickness and in health, to love and to cherish 'til death us do part."

You know, when you love someone, you don't need a gold star for being good to them. Just loving them is enough.

I finally decided to give up my gold star for good. I began to like the fact that we all had the same crowns, like we were a part of the same family. One day I approached the heavenly greeter with a new request.

> I've decided I don't need to see God for a while. Just tell him I understand now. I don't need a reward. I have only done what God wanted me to do, what he designed me to do. And that's enough.

God will like that, he said. *He will like that very much.*

Okay, can you leave heaven and come back to earth now?

I will confess, every once in a while I still have this craving for a big gold star. But I am going to try to live without one. So I'm leaving it here on the communion rail. I know that some of you are just dying to have it. You deserve it, right? But you might want to wait until the sanctuary clears out before picking it up.

But me? I'm going to try to live without it.

"I guess from now on, I'll just have to be good for nothing!"

SERMON OVERVIEW

Sermon Sentence: *Don't do good for the sake of earning gold stars; do it for nothing.*

Context: The congregation was beginning to work through their grief over the lost of their pastor. They needed to hear a new word, one not centered in the heaviness of death but from a different perspective.

Category of Sermon: *Expansion of a Parable* (Based on a parable but fleshed out in human experience.)

Sermon Form: An exploration of human behavior ending in a theological concept.

Techniques Used: Lots of humor based on human behavior. An imaginative ending staged in heaven. Use of phrase "good for nothing" as a theme and final punch line. Repetition of the central image—"gold star."

Purpose: To present a serious human flaw—expecting rewards for good behavior—and replacing it with a better theology. A second goal was to provide the congregation an opportunity to laugh. In addition, I would deal with the serious matter of my wife's illness but without signs of melancholy, modeling for them a healthy passage of grief.

Ending: I employed a delayed punch line, delivered as I was walking back to my seat. It was a line implied throughout the sermon—that we don't expect to do good without reward, or for "nothing." The ending had a fun double meaning, poking fun at myself: "I guess from now on I'll just have to be *good for nothing.*"

GENERAL COMMENTS

This sermon is one of my favorites. Yes, I do preach sermons more than once. But to repeat them does not make them "old." They are "old" only if they are *old* to the one who preaches them. (We don't keep our favorite life stories to ourselves, but tell them excitedly to new friends or acquaintances.) Oddly enough, it was a new ending that would give this sermon its most poignant aspect. I was preparing to preach this sermon and began to reflect on its application to my own life. I suddenly realized that there was one time I best "lived out" the message of the sermon—it was during my wife's twenty-seven month battle with cancer, when I was her caregiver. I decided to create an imaginative ending as the setting for my discovery, making the sharing less heavy. I preached the sermon with the new ending and it worked well for me and the congregation.

Several years later I was asked to pastor a church following the death of their senior pastor. This is the same church where I preached "Prayer: Beyond a Genie Mentality." But now it was time to leave the heavier issues of grief and questions of faith. Now was the time for the congregation to address other issues. I decided it was time for them to hear "Hey! Where's my Gold Star!" Why did they need this sermon at this time? I know it may sound superficial, but they needed to laugh. They had not laughed for years. Who can laugh watching your pastor die of cancer? Who can laugh going through grief? Yet the time had now come for laughter. And what more laughable subject can one choose than husbands thinking they deserve a gold star just for taking out the trash?

After I finished the sermon for the eleven o'clock service, the congregation exploded with spontaneous applause. Why the applause? Perhaps, in part, because it was a good sermon—at least one of my best. But I don't believe that is why they applauded. They clapped as a celebration. They clapped because they had been able to laugh. They applauded enthusiastically and when they did so, if was as though they had taken a deep breath and were now ready to move forward. The secret to the sermon's success was its timing. The applause told me the timing had been right, at least for most of them.

I could not have preached that sermon the first Sunday I arrived at that grieving church. It would have been rightly perceived as insensitive and in poor taste. My point is this: it is not just important *what* we preach but *when* we preach it. Timing is not everything, but it remains in the top ten.

CHAPTER TEN

LAST WORDS

A Spiritual Endeavor

After spending considerable time in the writing of this book, I am more convinced than ever that preaching is a craft to be honed. To be sure, it is not an exact science and technique is only part of a sermon's effectiveness. Dedication to the task is essential along with a pastor's heart. Preaching remains forever a covenantal partnership, never be undertaken alone, but always with the guidance of the Spirit.

An Awesome and Blessed Task

I will always be grateful that I was called into ministry and that the living out of that call included a weekly proclamation of God's word. For more than thirty-eight years the role of preaching was central to my maturation as a Christian and as a human being. Key to my growth was the demand that I study the Scriptures regularly and seek to understand them. An equal challenge was to become a student of life itself, discerning every aspect of the human spirit in the face of formidable challenges.

Through the years I took to heart an old saying, "practice what you preach." That mantra reminded me that every sermon—with all its insights and challenges—must be directed first to me, and only then to the congregation. The by-product of such a practice may well be both *authentic* preaching, and *authentic* living.

As I stand to preach, I always feel the weight of sharing God's word. It is only as I look back over the many years of preaching, however, that I can comprehend the great harvests of such sacred labor. I know now that without the disciplines and effort that excellent preaching requires, my life would be much reduced in its wisdom, compassion, and sense of purpose.

My hope is that every preacher who reads this book will experience both dimensions of the preaching task—its demands and its benefits. Preaching is, after all, an awesome responsibility and a blessed privilege.

APPENDIX

THE 10 COMMANDMENTS OF PREACHING
By Justin Tull

1. You shall seek to glorify God and not yourself.

2. You shall not promote the false gods and false teachings of the culture.

3. You shall not use the Lord's name in vain, preaching without passion or conviction.

4. Remember that preaching is a holy task. Always approach it with reverence.

5. Honor those of your congregation by remembering their doubts, their pain, their sin, and their value in God's eyes.

6. You shall not use the pulpit as a weapon or soap box.

7. You shall not pretend to be better than your congregation.

8. You shall not bear false witness to your people using the thoughts of others without giving credit to them.

9. You shall not preach to others without first speaking the words to yourself.

10. Practice what you preach. This is the only proper conclusion to a sermon.

RESOURCES FOR VITAL PREACHING

GENERAL TEXTS
Craddock, Fred B., *Preaching*
Eslinger, Richard L., *The Webb of Preaching*
Hamilton, Adam, *Unleashing the Word*
Long, Thomas G., *The Witness of Preaching*
Sparks, Lee and Kathryn, ed., *Craddock on the Craft of Preaching*
Taylor, Barbara Brown, *The Preaching Life*
Tull, Justin W., *Vital Preaching: the Art of Sharing God's Word*
Webb, Joseph M., *Preaching Without Notes*

ADDITIONAL RESOURCES:
Allen, Ronald J., *The Teaching Sermon*
Forbes, James, *The Holy Spirit and Preaching*
Holbert, John C. and McKenzie, Alyce, *What Not to Say*
Lowry, Eugene L, *The Sermon: Dancing on the Edge of Ministry*
McKenzie, Alyce M., *Preaching Biblical Wisdom in a Self-Help Society*
McKenzie, Alyce M., *Preaching Proverbs*
Mitchell, Henry H., *Celebration and Experience in Preaching*
O'Day, Gail R. and Long, Thomas G., ed., *Listening to the Word*

BOOKS OF SERMONS:
Claypool, John, *How to Handle Grief: Tracks of a Fellow Struggler*
Craddock, Fred B., *The Cherry Log Sermons*
Craddock, Fred B., *The Collected Sermons of Fred B. Craddock*
Gomes, Peter J., *Sermons: Biblical Wisdom for Daily Living*
Hamilton, Adam, *Confronting the Controversies*
Smedes, Lewis B., *How Can it be All Right When Everything is All Wrong?*
Taylor, Barbara Brown, *Home by Another Way*
Tull, Justin W., *Why God Why? Sermons on the Problem of Pain*

PRACTICE OF MINISTRY:
Carl III, William J., *Best Advice*
Niebuhr, Reinhold, *Leaves from the Notebook of a Tamed Cynic*
Tull, Justin, *Surviving and Thriving in Ministry*

ILLUSTRATIONS:
Graves, Mike and Ward, Richard F., ed., *Craddock Stories*
Remen, Rachael Naomi, *Kitchen Table Wisdom*

161

A LISTENER'S GUIDE FOR SERMONS

INTERN NAME _____   *DATE OF SERMON* _____

SCRIPTURE PASSAGE(S) _____

BEGINNING OF SERMON: What was helpful? What was not helpful?

BODY OF SERMON:

1. In a sentence or two, state what you heard as the central message of the sermon.

2. How well was the central message related to the scripture passage?

3. How well were you able to follow the preacher? What helped or distracted?

4. At which points did the sermon address <u>real</u> issues, both those with which you struggle and issues in the community and world?

5. What illustrative material did the sermon use? What images, metaphors, stories did the sermon offer?

CONCLUSION OF SERMON: What was the good news? How was the good news celebrated?

1. As you look at the preacher, describe your most prominent impression.

2. How did the delivery (voice, body language, style) <u>enhance</u> and <u>detract</u> from the message of the sermon?

3. How would you describe the preacher's own feelings about the sermon?

4. How did the sermon gain and maintain your attention?

5. How did the sermon engage your emotions?

RESPONSE:

1. How did your own opinions and beliefs fit or not fit with this sermon?

2. What did the sermon challenge you to do?

SUMMARY:

1. Share what you especially appreciated about this sermon.

2. Share suggestions you would give to the preacher for strengthening his/her preaching.

HEY! WHERE'S MY GOLD STAR?

FAVORITE PARABLE? Good Samaritan? Prodigal Son?
Today's Parable? Anyone pick this one?
We believe in rewards and consequences
We do something well, we expect credit, reward, praise!

THE GOLD STAR SYNDRONE
"For every good act there should be a reward"
Could we ever be truly good if this were the rule?

HUSBANDS OR WIVES? Who is worse about gold stars?
Man that takes garbage and wants a day of golf!
My father/ Lynn's father/ Andy Capp/ "bad husbands"

CHILDREN/ YOUTH Carrot/ stick? Helpful? backfire?
Cleaned my room/ McDonalds/ *Good grades*? Car at 16

SOCIETY I showed up/ deserve a raise
Football linemen/ beat chest/ $15,000 tackle
Children, youth, adults, doing what they should
"HEY, WHERE'S MY GOLD STAR?"

"No way, Jose!" Only did what you should have done

GOLD STAR FROM GOD/ Theological trap
How could God let this happen to me? I've been good.
Jesus condemned the Pharisees, the gold star seekers
"HEY GOD, WHERE'S MY GOLD STAR?"

IMAGINE HEAVEN "I made it!"
At the gate, Your name? Dr. Tull
No titles here. Just arrived. I'll call you *"Just in"*

REWARD? Where do I get my reward? No such word
Starry crown? I've been good/ minister for 37 years
Not reward. You only did what you were supposed to do

CROWN – finally got it, but everyone had one
Longer I stayed the better it felt/ being a part

REALIZATION time when gold stars not that important
Wife's illness better husband / didn't need much praise

VOW – in sickness and in health – till death us do part.
Give in love – no need for a reward!
I understand now. "Grace is a gift!"
"ANYONE NEED A GOLD STAR?"
I guess from now on, I'll just have to be. . .
GOOD FOR NOTHING!

Made in the USA
San Bernardino, CA
28 December 2017